VIRGIL MICHEL
American Catholic

R. W. Franklin, Robert L. Spaeth

D1592487

THE LITURGICAL PRESS
Collegeville, Minnesota 56321

THE LITURGICAL PRESS
Collegeville, Minnesota 56321

Cover design by Don Bruno.

The photos in this book are courtesy of the St. John's Abbey Archives.

Manufactured in the United States of America.

1	2	3	4	5	6	7	8	9

Library of Congress Cataloging-in-Publication Data

Franklin, R. W., 1947–
    Virgil Michel : American Catholic / R.W. Franklin, Robert Spaeth.
      p.   cm.
    ISBN 0-8146-1584-8 : $7.95
    1. Michel, Virgil George, 1890–1938. 2. Catholic Church—United
States—Clergy—Biography. 3. Liturgical movement—Catholic Church-
-History—20th century. 4. Catholic Church—Liturgy.   I. Spaeth,
Robert L. II. Title.
BX4705.M5512F73 1988
282′.092′4—dc19
[B]   88-10169
                                                    CIP

To
the Memory of
Michael Blecker, O.S.B.
(1931–1988)
Monk of St. John's Abbey
President of St. John's University
President of the Graduate Theological Union

Contents

Virgil Michel during 1933–1938 when he was editor of *Orate Fratres,* direc-tor of The Liturgical Press, and dean of St. John's University.

1

Virgil Michel and Our Times

Fifty years after the death of Virgil Michel, his life's work remains unfinished. Conventional wisdom would hold that today's major problems of Church and society differ drastically from those of the 1920s and 1930s, the period of Michel's creative efforts. But any survey of contemporary issues placed side-by-side with a list of those issues taken up by this monk of St. John's Abbey will instead show a remarkable congruence. Whether it be understanding and achieving social justice, or living a Christian life between the extremes of individualism and collectivism, or creating an authentic and effective Roman Catholic liturgy, or educating youth to a life of faith and reason—all such concerns were of great moment to Virgil Michel, and they are equally urgent for us, half a century later.

Nonetheless, one may legitimately wonder whether we and our contemporaries can learn anything significant about today's great unsolved problems from the life and writings of Virgil Michel. To be sure he addressed a Church and society rather different from our own. His age has passed; our own presses relentlessly upon us. What can a committed teacher, priest, and monk who responded to the world between the two world wars teach us who live in the nuclear age and the post-Vatican II Church? The answer that led to this book lies in the facts: idea after idea, essay after essay, project after project issuing from Virgil Michel speak across the years to today's Christians. And it is not only the issues that remain alive, but also Michel's analysis of them, as well as his suggested remedies for great problems, that ring true today.

A MONK OF THE WORLD

Although Father Virgil spent all of his adult life as a monk, he was fully engaged with worldly questions. Although a scholar, he did not restrict his efforts to scholarship. Nor could he be satisfied with a single discipline. He ranged restlessly over a wide spectrum of problems and projects, throwing his great energies into teaching, speaking, writing, editing, publishing, administration, and the creation of organizations to spread the ideas he believed in. When work needed to be done to further an important cause, Michel was available and willing to do it, sometimes to the detriment of his own health.

One of Michel's typical trips away from St. John's—during which he conferred, lectured, celebrated Mass, preached, and kept a diary—reveals the energy and dedication that characterize the man. This trip lasted from April 3–30, 1938; Virgil's destination was Nova Scotia, where he aimed to observe that Canadian province's cooperative and credit-union movement first-hand. On the train trip east from Collegeville, he stopped to lecture in Detroit and Niagara Falls, in Windsor, Canada, and then in Nova Scotia itself. After finishing his work there, he moved on to New York City, where he met with his publishers. Then to Annapolis, Maryland, to meet with the dean of St. John's College, Scott Buchanan, whom Michel wished to consult about that college's new program in liberal education. Along the way Virgil found time for some radio talks, for writing in his diary, for preaching and celebrating Mass, and for visiting some of his many friends. His itinerary reveals little or no free time.

At home or away, Father Virgil kept up a punishing pace of work. Little wonder that his health occasionally suffered or that he had to be held down by his superiors. Once in 1937 he had been asked to serve as the secretary of the International Academy of Christian Sociologists. In reply, Virgil wrote, "I know without asking Father Abbot that he will definitely say no because he has given me orders in regard to accepting further work. . . ."

In Michel's approach to his work, his contemporaries saw a special zeal. One acute observer was the Baroness Catherine de Hueck, who in her search for interracial justice founded Friendship Houses, first in Toronto, later in New York and other American cities. Years after Michel's death, the Baroness recalled him as he appeared in the early 1930s: "He was young, but he was carrying a flame within him. . . . Perhaps I mean fire, the fire that renews the face of the earth."[1]

From the two decades of Virgil Michel's productive work, we have inherited a legacy in half-a-dozen critical areas, including philosophy, liturgy, social justice, economic life, education, and the role of the laity in the Church. Nor were these separate areas of inquiry and action for Michel; he attacked the problems and the needs of people with all of the tools available to him in the Church and in secular thought.

TIMES OF CRISIS

At the beginning of his professional life, Virgil Michel faced a world reeling from the slaughter of World War I. Violence had wrecked many of Europe's communities and undermined belief in the decency and efficacy of Western culture. But the peace of the 1920s that ensued brought a new rush to materialism in the West, particularly in the United States. Collectivism in the form of Soviet communism threatened to disrupt life still more, and soon the totalitarianism of fascist Italy and Nazi Germany posed equally serious threats.

The 1930s opened with the world sliding into the Great Depression, showing that poverty as well as materialist prosperity can have devastating effects on community life. Could it be that Christians had to stand not only against communism and fascism, but also against capitalism?

Little wonder then that Virgil Michel's work and writings are redolent of crisis—crisis in economics and politics, crisis in religion and the Church, crisis in the human soul. His was a time of crisis, and Michel believed that the message of the Gospel had to address the critical issues of the day and assist people who suffered from the depredations of their times.

Ours is a time of crisis also. And although some of the terms of the crisis have changed, many of the threats and grave problems Virgil Michel discerned remain or have intensified. Communism and capitalism still compete for allegiance, both in the international arena, and—in philosophical forms of collectivism and individualism—in the human person. Although fascism was crushed in World War II, its grim reminder of the depths to which the human animal can descend hovers over the world to this day.

After World War II prosperity returned to the West, and with it a new round of materialism threatened to eat away once again at the spirituality of Christians and others. Moreover, the prosperity of the industrialized societies makes more stark the poverty of the Third World, and the competition of capitalism and communism makes the desperation of the poor an explosive factor in humanity's quest for stability and peace.

How can the world's harsh crises be addressed by Christianity, whose primary teaching is love? How shall Christians respond to the claims and conquests of political, economic, and philosophical ideologies? Is there hope in education? If so, what kind of education? Does the tradition of social thought in the Catholic Church offer answers to questions raised by the crisis conditions of the world? Does the Church itself, in its life of worship, provide a model for human life more in line with human dignity than the models offered by others? These questions need our attention no less than they needed Virgil Michel's. And as in Michel's time, when one question is addressed, it leads on to others.

INDIVIDUALISM

Instructive insight into Virgil Michel's thought, as well as into the issues of today, can be gained through the concept of individualism, so central to American life and history. Indeed, this American phenomenon was so significant for Father Virgil's work that it has been selected as the main theme of this book.

In an essay published in 1936, Michel declared that individualism can be understood as either something good or something bad. In its good sense he said the term individualism "stands for appreciation of human personality, for the development and promotion of individual traits or individual characteristics or individual elements in human nature and personality."[2]

Had Michel believed modern American society to be individualistic in this way and this way only, he probably would not have stressed a second characteristic of individualism— "the bad sense." This side of individualism, in Michel's words, "has as its supreme principle that every individual not only should think for himself and judge for himself, but that he is ultimately his own standard for everything."[3]

Individualism in both its aspects has important effects on society. Michel said:

> The good effect of individualism is that it fosters a spirit of enterprise, self-activity, self-reliance, responsibility, and therefore initiative, originality and resourcefulness.
> The bad effect of individualism is above all that it fosters a ruthless pursuit of self-interest, egoism, and makes out of human life a bitter, cutthroat competition for existence and for improvement of one's own condition over against all others.[4]

Individualism in Michel's "good sense" is readily recognized as the American ideal; in the "bad sense" he and other critics of American life saw a large part of American reality. Michel saw the latter aspect of individualism to be dangerous to the common good, and he saw the danger spreading throughout economic life, government, ethics, and even religion.

In the half-century since Virgil Michel's time, individualism has increased its influence among Americans, for good and ill. Today we cannot understand American society without understanding this fact, much less analyze our society's problems or find remedies for them. Virgil Michel's accomplishments will contribute much to our understanding.

SOCIAL JUSTICE

If not individualism, then what principle ought to govern society? Virgil Michel's answer was "social justice." In a 1937 essay Michel proposed that social justice is "properly defined as the virtue by which men regulate all their actions in proper relation to the common good."[5] And what is the common good? Michel affirmed "the traditional Christian concept of the common good, which is based on the concept of the social nature of man together with an emphatic acceptance of the supreme value of human personality."[6]

For Michel, two distinct conditions in society were necessary before one could say that the common good was being served. The first he called "the common conditions of social life" such as "social organization, peace and order, opportunities of education, of work, of self-development, freedom for the higher things in life, etc."[7] The second is "the maximum attainment of the good life by all individuals," which must be achieved by the individuals themselves; therefore, "the fundamental rights of all . . . must always be respected, in fact guaranteed, by any common action or attitude of the whole."[8]

Should we interpret Virgil Michel's support of social justice and his critique of individualism only in relation to societal conditions during the Great Depression of the 1930s, the era in which he produced these thoughts? Or do his ideas apply to our society as well? Have the problems he saw in American individualism disappeared as a result of progress from the 1930s to the 1980s?

The American Catholic bishops in their 1986 pastoral letter *Economic Justice for All* analyze American society, at least
its economy, in terms very similar to Virgil Michel's. The
bishops identify "social fragmentation" as one of the undesir-
able results of the industrial revolution's stress on the "divi-
sion of labor into specialized jobs and professions." They also
deplore the "decline in seeing how one's work serves the whole
community, and an increased emphasis on personal goals and
private interests."[9] The proper moral basis for economic life,
according to the American bishops, is expressed in this principle: "The dignity of the human person, realized in community with others, is the criterion against which all aspects of
economic life must be measured."[10] Although the words are
somewhat different, the meaning of this principle is virtually
identical with Virgil Michel's understanding of social justice.

One explanation for the remarkable congruence of Michel's
thought with that of today's Catholic bishops derives from the
fact that they both stand in the twentieth-century tradition of
Catholic social thought; Michel and the bishops are devoted
to the social encyclicals of the popes since Leo XIII. But this
explanation needs to be supplemented by the remarkable fact
that the bishops of the 1980s recognize that economic society
today stands in need of the same moral analysis as Michel gave
to American society in the 1930s. Michel opposed a corrosive
individualism; the bishops, in harmony with this analysis, suggest that the proper outlook in economic life is "solidarity,"
which they define as "another name for [the] social friendship
and civic commitment that make human moral and economic
life possible."[11]

To Virgil Michel, individualism represented an extreme response to the challenge of community life. Collectivism, especially in its totalitarian forms, represented another extreme.
The goal of traditional social justice was for him a middle way.
How this middle way can be realized, how the temptations
of the extremes can be avoided, how the Church can contribute to the realization of a just society—these are questions

treated extensively by Virgil Michel as well as by religious thinkers of our day.

This book surveys Michel's thought in several areas, aiming to understand his approach, to appreciate his statement of problems and his recommended solutions, to relate his thought to our contemporary crises. Individualism as a challenge and a problem runs as a thread through the book's entire fabric.

LITURGY

One persistent theme in Virgil Michel's thought exemplifies both his approach and the need to bring his thought into the 1980s and beyond. That is the function of Christian liturgy in the life of a community.

Then as now, any mention of liturgy in connection with such vast problems as materialism or poverty is greeted with skepticism. Michel admitted as much when he opened a 1935 essay by asking, "Can the liturgy help to give jobs or raise wages?"[12] To reach an answer to this question, Michel reviewed the dangers of individualism and collectivism, and offered a solution of moderation, of balancing—a Christian spirit that takes into account both the individual and the social sides of human nature.

Here Michel followed the lead of Pope Pius XI, whose encyclical of 1931, *Quadragesimo anno*, said that "social reconstruction must be preceded by a profound renewal of the Christian spirit."[13] And where does a Christian turn to find the sources of this Christian spirit? Michel answered: the liturgy.

The basic idea of the liturgy of the Catholic Church, Michel argued, is the doctrine of the Mystical Body of Christ, a doctrine teaching mutual interdependence of all members of the Church. With Christ as the head, this body, the Church, Michel wrote in 1935, "is the highest type of Christian solidarity—a supernatural living solidarity or fellowship—not only in theory but also in practice."[14] As the Church teaches that we the people are interdependent under Christ, so it exemplifies that solidarity in its public worship.

Michel quoted the great British historian of Catholic culture Christopher Dawson in order to make a central point about the liturgy of the Church: Michel was confident that since liturgical worship is "a visible united action on the part of the members" of the church, so the members "cannot fail to revive and foster in them a determination to carry their Christ-life into the social and economic sphere."[15]

The crucial importance of the liturgy moved Virgil Michel to a long and determined campaign to reform the worship of the Roman Catholic Church, to make it more effective in people's daily lives. Through The Liturgical Press and *Orate Fratres* magazine (now *Worship*), and by means of energetic writing and teaching, and with the help of his confreres at St. John's Abbey—all of this activity summed up in the term "the liturgical movement"—Virgil Michel labored for a renewal of Catholic worship that was only realized after his death, at Vatican Council II.

The Constitution on the Sacred Liturgy of Vatican II can be understood in many ways as a vindication of Michel's work for liturgical reform. Michel's own convictions are directly echoed in passages from the conciliar document such as, "Mother Church earnestly desires that all the faithful should be led to that full, conscious, and active participation in liturgical celebrations which is demanded by the very nature of the liturgy." In words very similar to those often used by Michel, the Council fathers characterized the liturgy as "the primary and indispensable source from which the faithful are to derive the true Christian spirit."[16]

Yet the emphasis Virgil Michel repeatedly gave to the connection of the Church's liturgy with social justice—as in the title of his 1935 essay "The Liturgy the Basis of Social Regeneration"—is not stressed in the Vatican II document on the liturgy. Nor can it be claimed that the post-Vatican II liturgical reforms have led to the effects in society that Michel expected a renewed liturgy to have. Certainly Christians, and Catholics in particular, have in recent years become more socially conscious than in the past, but the effectiveness of Christian liturgy in encouraging and guiding this consciousness remains problematic. Hence the need to investigate once again the analysis of the liturgy-social justice connection so strongly urged by Virgil Michel.

EDUCATION

If Christians are to be guided by the liturgy, they must understand it and its theological underpinnings. To this end Michel devoted time and thought to the religious education of young people in elementary and secondary schools. From 1929 he collaborated with the Dominican sisters of Marywood in Grand Rapids, Michigan, writing with the sisters a series of religion textbooks. These became the Christ-Life Series for grade schools and the Christian Religion Series for high schools.

An indication of how important Father Virgil considered this catechetical work to be can be gleaned from a letter he wrote in 1935 to the *Catholic Educational Review*. Commenting on the Christ-Life Series, he said, "This Series represents intense labor for at least seven years and much classroom experience. It is the only thing I continued to work at while I was up at the Indian Missions on account of health."

These texts, emphasizing training in the liturgy, were written for pupils in Catholic schools. Today the challenge for catechesis has changed, for the proportion of Catholic children attending parochial schools has decreased radically from the 1930s. Today the spirit of Virgil Michel must be infused into Confraternity of Christian Doctrine (CCD) programs, into parish instruction programs, and into children's training within the family. The challenge of religious education has become much more difficult since Virgil Michel's time.

Michel concentrated even more energy, both theoretical and practical, on higher education. From early in his career he taught at St. John's University—courses in English and philosophy—and for the last five years of his life he was also dean of the University. In the 1930s he designed and taught a two-year course on Catholic social thought, for which he drew up an extensive syllabus, drawing on the best and most progressive European Catholic thinkers.

From time to time he wrote articles and gave speeches on the purposes of college education; one of his major efforts of this kind appeared in 1926, entitled "Utopia Rediviva." Here he criticized the current stress on utilitarian education and advocated a "cultural education" for all students. He asserted that to teach culture was to be as modern as to teach utility. This "modern cultural course" would include the natural sciences, mathematics, "history in all its wider human aspects," the classics, philosophy. He wanted this education to avoid the superficiality of the typical survey course: "The course must go deeper and attempt to get more down to the bottom of problems . . . to the end of things. . . ."[17]

American colleges today are perhaps more utilitarian and more superficial than those criticized by Virgil Michel in the 1920s and 1930s. To rouse them from bad habits will once again require the wisdom and drive that Michel exhibited in his own time. Catholic colleges in particular struggle today to discover their identity within the Church, thus adding a special problem to those remaining from Michel's era.

THE LAITY

Michel's thoughts about Catholic education naturally related to the role of the laity in the Church. He deplored the possibility that in a Church led by a strong clergy, lay people might be understood as "a spiritual proletariat" whose only responsibility would be "passive obedience like the chess pawn . . . moved to the right or the left."[18]

As early as 1929, Michel's convictions about an active role for the laity were strong. Writing to George Schuster, the managing editor of *Commonweal* magazine, Virgil added an impassioned postscript: "Some day an 'official teacher' will have to re-utter the age-old Catholic doctrine that the layfolk are not merely trained dogs but true living members of the Church and in their own way true apostles of Christ!"

For Michel, the lay apostolate and the liturgical spirit went hand in hand; passivity in the liturgy unfortunately went well with passivity in the worldly duties of the Christian, with deplorable results.

Vatican Council II again proved Michel's ideas prophetic, particularly in its Decree on the Apostolate of Lay People of 1965. The lay apostolate, the Council fathers wrote, "is something that derives from the layman's very vocation as a Christian."[19] Just as Virgil Michel would have said, the Council also made clear: "The laity are made to share in the priestly, prophetical and kingly office of Christ" particularly "when they endeavor to have the Gospel spirit permeate and improve the temporal order."[20]

In the decades since Vatican II Catholics around the world have been struggling to understand and to put the Council's ideas on the laity into practice. The task is by no means complete, nor is it clear that progress is always being made. In this area as in so many others, a return to Virgil Michel, to an understanding of his life and writings, holds out hope for us and our contemporaries.

When modern Christians ask, "To whom can we turn for help in facing the crises of our lives and our world?" it is perfectly proper to answer, "The Church." But that answer is also inadequate. The post-Vatican II Church contains many voices, often competing for the attention of its thoughtful, worried members. This book constitutes a recommendation that the voice of Virgil Michel is worth attending to, despite the fact that he lived his life long before the Council. Virgil Michel always spoke in the Gospel spirit, and he was ever determined to infuse worldly matters with that spirit. His voice was above all a clear one; much of its clarity can help us today to penetrate the confusions surrounding us.

NOTES

1. Catherine de Hueck Doherty, *Not Without Parables: Stories of Yesterday, Today and Eternity* (Notre Dame, Ind.: Ave Maria Press, 1972) 104.

2. Virgil Michel, "Individualism and Its Social Effects," in Robert L. Spaeth, ed., *The Social Question: Essays on Capitalism and Christianity* (Collegeville: St. John's University, 1987) 10.

3. Michel, "Individualism and Its Social Effects," *ibid.* 9–10.

4. Michel, "Individualism and Its Social Effects," *ibid.* 10.

5. Virgil Michel, "The Common Good," in Robert L. Spaeth, ed., *The Social Question* 24.

6. Michel, "The Common Good," *ibid.* 26.

7. Michel, "The Common Good," *ibid.* 26.

8. Michel, "The Common Good," *ibid.* 27.

9. National Conference of Catholic Bishops, *Economic Justice for All: Pastoral Letter on Catholic Social Teaching and the U.S. Economy* (Washington: United States Catholic Conference, 1986) para. 22.

10. *Economic Justice for All* para. 28.

11. *Economic Justice for All* para. 66.

12. Virgil Michel, "The Liturgy the Basis of Social Regeneration," in Robert L. Spaeth, ed., *The Social Question* 1.

13. Quoted in Michel, "The Liturgy the Basis of Social Regeneration," *ibid.* 4.

14. Michel, "The Liturgy the Basis of Social Regeneration," *ibid.* 6.

15. Quoted in Michel, "The Liturgy the Basis of Social Regeneration," *ibid.* 8.

16. "The Constitution on the Sacred Liturgy," in Austin Flannery, ed., *Vatican Council II: The Conciliar and Post Conciliar Documents* (Collegeville: The Liturgical Press, 1975) para. 14.

17. Virgil Michel, "Utopia Rediviva," in Robert L. Spaeth, ed., *Liberal Education: Essays on the Philosophy of Higher Education* (Collegeville: St. John's University, 1981) 17–18.

18. Quoted in Paul B. Marx, *Virgil Michel and the Liturgical Movement* (Collegeville: The Liturgical Press, 1957) 192.

19. "Decree on the Apostolate of Lay People," in Austin Flannery, ed., *Vatican Council II* para. 1.

20. "Decree on the Apostolate of Lay People," *ibid.* para. 2.

2

Virgil Michel and His Times

In 1988 we commemorate the fiftieth anniversary of Virgil Michel's death, and we approach the centenary of his birth, for he was born in 1890 and died in 1938. Michel was raised in a large Catholic family in St. Paul, Minnesota, attending grade school at Assumption School in St. Paul and high school at St. John's Preparatory School in Collegeville, Minnesota. He entered the novitiate of St. John's Abbey in 1909, professed his solemn monastic vows in 1913, and remained a Benedictine monk for the final twenty-five years of his life.

At the time of his sudden death at age forty-eight, contemporary observers were dazzled by Virgil Michel as a man of almost universal talents: a violinist in the St. John's orchestra; a star of baseball and tennis; a Benedictine monk and priest; an English and philosophy professor; a coach of prep school athletics; the founder of *Orate Fratres* magazine and The Liturgical Press; a translator, a lecturer, a college administrator, an ecumenist; a writer of books, pamphlets, and articles on worship, social justice, peace, race relations, economics, philosophy, art, architecture, education, and literature. All of these phrases described Virgil Michel in 1938.

Fifty years later we can see always in the mainstream of Virgil Michel's life three goals: the rediscovery of the social mission of the Roman Catholic Church, the revival of liturgical worship, and the renewal of Catholic education in the United States. The central factor binding these three features, social justice, worship, and education, into one whole was the ideal of community. All of Virgil Michel's work was united in one endeavor: the restoration of the communal dimension of American Catholicism. Early Christianity had assumed the community as a given, whereas in the American culture of Michel's time the individual was the given and the community appeared as the task to be achieved. The venerable tradition of Christian fellowship in Church and society had receded far into the background.

INDIVIDUALISM IN HISTORY

The story of Western civilization as the progressive liberation of the individual has been at the heart of the historical consciousness of Europe and America for half a millennium. The drift toward the dominant individualism Virgil Michel opposed was undergirded by a number of long-term factors. The Italian Renaissance, the period of transition from the Middle Ages to modern times, put the individual at the center of intellectual and artistic inquiry. Renaissance humanists fostered a deep appreciation of private life and the retirement of the gentleman scholar from the concerns of the world. The leading early Italian humanist Petrarch advised his students to be true only to themselves. At the same time secular wealth and improved economic conditions in the flourishing cities of Germany and northern Europe made for a public emphasis on private pursuits. English university humanists of the sixteenth century focused on the dignity and worth of the individual and reveled in the image of the solitary autonomous hero.

The Enlightenment of the eighteenth century advanced this Renaissance goal of emancipating the human personality from ecclesiastical and political collectives. Enlightened *philosophes* summoned the individual to greater freedom and independence, and the works of *philosophes* such as Voltaire, with their ingrained antipathy to corporate religion, are the foundations of modern democratic liberalism.

In the name of the freedom of the individual, political revolutionaries in the eighteenth and nineteenth centuries broke up traditional secular and religious communities, such as artisan and commercial guilds, peasant farm communes, town corporations, and monastic and charitable associations. By 1830 revolutionaries had destroyed 98 percent of the monasteries of Europe. Nations founded on the political ideology of individualism were so hostile to any communal expression of religion that by 1845 only 5 percent of the prerevolutionary monastic houses of Europe had been restored.

It was in the United States that individualism became a concept of immense significance expressing all that has at various times been contained within the American dream: the philosophy of natural rights and the belief in free enterprise. Individualism is the word above all others which expressed the ideals of nineteenth- and twentieth-century America. It points to the realization in a New World of a new level of human progress in a society of equal rights, *laissez-faire* economics, and equal opportunity for all.

For the American philosopher Ralph Waldo Emerson, individualism was the only sure means for the creation of a social order of self-determined, self-reliant, and fully responsible citizens. Emerson wrote on the eve of the United States Civil War, "The Union is only perfect when all the uniters are isolated. Each man, if he attempts to join himself to others, is on all sides cramped and diminished. The Union must be ideal in actual individualism."[1]

The industrial revolution, the replacement of human labor by machines which reshaped American and European life through the early twentieth century, also advanced the separation of the individual from the community. In the name of free enterprise and self-help, the industrial revolution led to the dismantling of centuries of protective regulation in trade, to the removal of apprenticeship laws governing child labor, to the abolition of wage controls, and to the disappearance of the small workshop. The discipline of the new factory uprooted children and adults from their home communities. Until 1900 it was not uncommon in America for a child of six to be found working alone twelve hours a day before a machine. Society in the new industrial nations like the United States was divided by the great gulf of mass poverty, for the working class did not share in the increased wealth or the power over life that the industrial revolution had wrought.

Individualism was the keystone of the industrial age in America and Europe into which Virgil Michel was born. Capitalists extolled individual prowess. The literature of Virgil Michel's time brims over with "self-help," "self-reliance," "useful knowledge," "captains of industry." The leader of the influential Manchester School of free enterprise, Richard Cobden, was suspicious of general ideas especially when they involved some mystical, collective, or common good. "Mine is that masculine species of charity," Cobden wrote, "which would lead me to inculcate in the minds of the laboring classes the love of independence, the privilege of self-respect, the disdain of being patronized or petted, the desire to accumulate, and the ambition to rise."[2]

Individualism shows through the culture of the industrial age in a hundred different places: in the love of biographies and autobiographies; in the predominance of novels of character and worldly success; in the twentieth-century American city where hundreds of thousands of all classes crowded by one another as though they had nothing in common but the brutal indifference, the unfeeling isolation of each person in private interests and narrow self-seeking.

In a parallel manner, religious life in the Catholic Church tended increasingly to emphasize the individual and neglect the community after the sixteenth century. Religion was considered as something within; faith became a private matter; and worship was cut off from daily affairs and relegated to the strictly spiritual plane.

In worship in particular Catholics were unaware of themselves as a community. Because of the sixteenth-century controversy with the Protestant Reformers, the whole stress of Catholic thought on the Eucharist or Mass, and worship in general, was clerical and individualistic. The assembled congregation had no active voice in the Mass prayers at all. Divine service was celebrated in an unknown tongue; the cup was denied the laity at Communion; watching and hearing had become the only role of the faithful in the assembly. Consequently, popular pastoral practice pictured the Eucharist as a way of piety for the individual soul, rather than as a community action. Church interiors were fragmented and divided by symbols of status and class, and it was not uncommon to find glass partitions installed between seats for the poor and seats for the rich worshipers. Prelates were not disturbed that throughout the world from the sixteenth century until Virgil Michel's day the Catholic laity had little idea of what happened at a high Mass, did not sing at Mass, and avoided the Divine Office, the official daily prayer of the Church.

The interest of the early Fathers of the Church in the relationship between the "sacramental body of Christ" on the altar and the "Mystical Body of Christ" reflected in the fellowship of the faithful gathered about the altar had also been forgotten in Virgil Michel's time. A book that tried to restore Paul's and Augustine's teaching on the people as the "Body of Christ" had been condemned by the Council of Basle as "offensive to pious ears," a judgment which could not be repealed at Vatican Council I in 1871.[3] The Church was conceived primarily in terms of its hierarchical and political structures, not as a fellowship of the People of God. For example, in the seventeenth century the Jesuit theologian Robert Bellarmine had nurtured the ideal of Christian unity in the absolute monarchy of the papacy. To be a Christian was to be a subject of the sovereignty of the Pope. Bellarmine perceived the Church as a militant "perfect society" of ordered ranks "like the kingdom of France or the Republic of Venice."⁴

What was the place of the laity in this society? A nineteenth-century cardinal defined it this way: "The layman has two positions in the Church. He kneels before the altar; that is one. And he sits below the pulpit; that is another." Then the cardinal added that there is a third: "The layman also puts his hand into his pocket."⁵

THE CRY FOR COMMUNITY

Growing like a mighty wave through the nineteenth and early twentieth centuries, a second vital theme began to emerge: the cry for a return to the ideal of the human community in the Church and in secular society. As the social order that had been in existence for over a thousand years in Western civilization came to an end with the spread of mechanical power and the displacement of monarchy, and as weak human beings were seen to stand isolated before the monoliths of secular state, business, and industry, there was a rising protest against the impersonality of modern life of "fractional man," "irrational man," "mass man," "the face in the crowd," "the lonely individual."⁶

A new cultural dynamic appeared in America and Europe as a cluster of parallel movements in politics, the arts, and labor relations arose opposing the individualizing tendencies of the democratic and industrial revolutions. These were the times and this was the context in which Virgil Michel's life must be understood.

Karl Marx made the most famous secular political protest in the name of community. For him the crisis of individualism was symbolized by distressing scenes of misery and poverty in the new factory towns of the nineteenth century. The bourgeois emphasis on the free citizen to Marx had led to a dehumanized individual cut adrift because it had left no bond between men and women except "naked self-interest," "callous cash-payment," and "the icy waters of egotistical calculation."[7]

For Marx, the only possible way to emancipate humankind from the incubus of greed was to create one economic "community with others," and the means to this end was for the working class to carry out a single great, violent, worldwide revolution.[8] And so in 1864 he launched the International Workingmen's Association, later the Communist Party, to achieve the political goal of building community through revolution. By the time Virgil Michel first visited Europe in 1924, seven years after the Russian Revolution, the Soviet Union had become the first modern society to attempt social reconstruction by focusing on human interests alone, deliberately excluding transcendent factors from consideration.

The search for community within literary, musical, and artistic movements in the last 150 years is another part of the general attempt to achieve a communal revival in a rapidly modernizing society. Richard Wagner envisioned that his musical dramas at Bayreuth would demonstrate organic unity in a fragmented German society. As he passed through Germany, Virgil Michel could see Nazi Party rallies, shaped by Wagner's theories, which celebrated a totalitarian order which the Nazis imagined could be built up in modern Europe through an escape into art, through the embrace of the mysteries of a German national religion, or through the abandonment of the values of Western humanism.

Rudyard Kipling is an example of an English novelist of this period who maintained a sustained protest against a culture alienated from the ideal of community. To Kipling, Chicago was the great symbol of the crisis of individualism: "I have struck a city, a real city, and they call it Chicago. Having seen it I urgently desire never to see it again. It is inhabited by savages. Its air is dirt. I spent ten hours in that huge wilderness, wandering through scores of miles of these terrible streets. It was like watching a fool play with buttons."[9]

For the Modern Movement in architecture, from the Englishmen John Ruskin and William Morris through the German Bauhaus of the 1920s, it was "the great cry that rises from all our manufacturing cities, louder than their furnace blast— that we manufacture everything except men" that was the call to action for artists and builders, a call to translate principles of Gothic communalism into a modern style appropriate for an industrial civilization.[10] The Modern Movement maintained that collective art makes social integration possible and in 1923 Walter Gropius, speaking for the Bauhaus group, expressed the emerging ideal of community in terms of architecture: "The idea of a contemporary world is already recognized. The old dualistic world-picture which showed the individual in opposition to society is losing ground. In its place is rising the idea of a universal unity in which all opposing forces exist in a state of community."[11] By the 1930s when Virgil Michel began writing on Christian art, secular architects were teaching that communistic order would be restored out of the chaos of industrialism by embracing the materialism of the technical world.

VIRGIL MICHEL'S CALL

Virgil Michel was at one with all these critics in believing that a great judgment had come upon individualism, and for him that judgment was the economic Depression which began in the United States in the fall of 1929. Virgil Michel looked out from Minnesota across a land grown hard, cynical, and sinister. One-fourth of American families were on relief. The number of the unemployed had reached 15,000,000 by March 1933, and these developments touched a large number of American Roman Catholics in a disproportionate degree.

The Depression revealed to Father Virgil the naked dehumanization of a system founded on individualism, and he wrote that "all who can see with the eyes of the spirit cannot but be horrified at the corruption underneath."[12] The suffer-

ing caused by the Depression must lead Christians to question more than the causes of unemployment. It should lead
to a religious inquiry into the whole quality of life in the United
States, and of this Virgil Michel wrote in the 1930s:

> The greatest of the evils is perhaps the depersonalization of
> man, the reduction of man to a mere cog in a machine. The
> greatest evil of bourgeois capitalism is the harm it has done
> to man himself, to dehumanize and depersonalize man most
> completely.[13]

The significance of Virgil Michel lies in the fact that he
joined a critique of individualism which he held in common
with the wave of secular reformers in Europe and America to
a religious solution for the problems of society. A solution to
the social crisis was not just a matter of economics, politics,
or art. Here is where Christianity could make an indispensable contribution to the renewal of Western civilization and
to the quality of American life. The answer to the social question was to be found in the realm of the spirit, in the discovery of a "new Catholicism."

THE NEW CATHOLICISM

Most secular reformers in politics, the arts, and literature
looked upon Churches and religion as more or less archaic
hangovers from the past, destined, like warfare, to fade away
in the light of reason and social progress. In the nineteenth
century Catholicism was on the defensive as a moral and political force, threatened not only by secularism and science but
also by Marxism and other challenges to its authority. In Virgil Michel's time the Roman Catholic Church had survived,
not just in the service of those intractable mysteries and worship which eluded Marx and the secularists, but also in some
parts of the world itself now shaped powerfully by the new
cultural dynamic, the revival of community.

In 1842 the great Bavarian Church historian J.J.I. Döllinger
recognized the spirit of a "new Catholicism" emerging in a num-

ber of parallel Christian movements of his time. Döllinger wrote that "everything with us" points more and more distinctly "towards a drawing together of kindred elements."[14]

The "new Catholicism" means the Catholicism of modern times gradually taking shape in the nineteenth and twentieth centuries which restored the communal dimension of Christianity while never rejecting the hierarchical dimension of the Church. What were the "kindred elements" drawing together during the century which separated Döllinger from Virgil Michel that refined "the new Catholicism"?

First, an entirely new note was sounded in theology and worship. "The people" had become a primary association of the Church. Theology had gradually moved from juridical concepts such as "perfect society" to defining the Church, clergy and laity alike, as "one people." There was a renewed sense that God calls the whole of humanity to become God's daughters and sons: God's purpose is that all should share in the fellowship and worship of the Church. The corporate character of Catholic worship and witness began to spring from a wider grasping of the Church as one community, the Body of Christ. In the century before Virgil Michel, Catholic thought was driven more and more by the insight that God's creative and redemptive work in the world is intended to bring all of humankind into one community. How to realize this wider unity of the human family became one of the pressing tasks of the Roman Catholic Church.

THE CONTRIBUTION OF MÖHLER

In Germany a century before Virgil Michel's time, there had appeared a young teacher at the University of Tübingen, Johann Adam Möhler (1796–1838). Möhler was the first Roman Catholic theologian for a thousand years to argue that the ground of the Church was not the clergy or the state but the communal life of all believers.

Möhler beheld Christianity not as rules and dogma but as a life lived in common. His definition of the Church as a corporate unity, rather than as a legal or clerical entity, is based on his concept of the incarnation. Jesus continues to dwell on earth in his Church. Christ touches the world through the members of the Church; they are his agents for forging bonds of human unity.

Until 1838 Möhler campaigned in Germany against private Masses, for he was concerned that such non-communal worship by priests alone introduced a magical element into Christianity. He called for a return of the Communion cup to lay people at Mass, and he mocked nineteenth-century arguments that the language of the liturgy should be Latin because of its antiquity and its ability to transmit unity to the Church: "Such a unity! A unity based on ignorance and as for antiquity, why not use Hebrew in the liturgy? It is even older. Let the people understand their prayers."[15]

By relating the liturgy and the sacraments to the essential corporate nature of the Church, Möhler found a way to overcome the extremely individualized Roman Catholic sacramental theology generally current after the Reformation in such a way that his thinking stands behind the work of those theologians who fashioned a revised understanding of the relationship of the laity to the Church at Vatican Council II. All the great theologians who prepared the way for the restoration of the lay, communal dimension of the Roman Catholic Church at Vatican II, from Cardinal Joseph Ratzinger to Hans Küng, have admitted some debt to Johann Adam Möhler. Rarely in history has an Ecumenical Council owed so much to one man. In the documents of Vatican II, such as *Lumen gentium* and *Gaudium et spes*, the great mystery of the Church as a royal priestly people pilgrimaging in time can be expressed in no more fitting terminology than Möhler's phrase "the Church as the Body of Christ."[16]

THE CONTRIBUTION OF GUÉRANGER

In a parallel manner a French contemporary of Möhler's, Prosper Guéranger (1805–1875), felt called to a liturgical vocation in 1829 and refounded the Benedictine priory of Solesmes in 1833 as a center of Christian revitalization. Guéranger believed that in the advanced secularism of France a revival of Christianity could only be achieved through the restoration of the Church as an institution with a marked emphasis on the liturgy, the official cycle of Catholic worship. Guéranger first used the phrase "liturgical movement" in 1851 to define the rediscovery of the centrality of the Eucharist or Mass in the life and teaching of the Churches and to describe a campaign for the full and active participation of the Catholic laity in frequent celebrations of the Eucharist. In time the refounding of Solesmes came to be seen as the first stage in the awakening of the liturgical sense for the Catholic world.

It is important to consider Guéranger with Virgil Michel because the chief contribution of the French Benedictine to the modern Church was the rediscovery of the liturgy as a Christian instrument for the destruction of individualism. Guéranger taught very clearly that the Eucharist is both the praise of God and the means for being incorporated into a human community, the Church. His most intriguing sentences in the introduction to *The Liturgical Year* (1841) emphasize above all that the social dimension of prayer is the basis for all true worship and that the Eucharist is a common offering, the work of all the people, in which the assembly of the laity must unite in the closest possible manner with everything that is said and done by the priest at the altar.

In time Guéranger's liturgical revival became one source that led on to a general renewal of the Catholic Church. The restoration of the communal dimension of Catholicism was the most significant achievement of Vatican Council II (1962–1965). The documents of the Council point out how profoundly Christianity is a communion of people together with

God. To the Council, social conscience reflects the communal dimension of human beings that is brought to fulfillment in the Church understood as the Body of Christ.

Another prominent idea of the Council is that the primary means of living the Christian life is active participation in Eucharistic worship, not by the clergy alone but also by laymen and laywomen as well. This new understanding of the Church at Vatican II, expressed in the 1960s and 1970s in a global emphasis upon communal forms of worship: the liturgy, Eucharistic Communion, and the liturgical year, rather than on individual acts of piety: the Rosary, private prayer or sermons, has transformed the face of Christendom, in the shift of altars from distant sanctuaries into the midst of actively participating congregations and in the style of the great new public edifices, like the Liverpool Catholic Cathedral, which was the first round cathedral to be built since the ninth century. The sound of Catholicism has changed, too, for within all these structures Mass has been celebrated in the language of the people for the first time in a thousand years.

AMERICAN PROPHET

The prism of the past turns, and now, half a century after his death and in the light of these developments, Virgil Michel must be seen as the first twentieth-century American prophet of the new Catholicism. The historic mission of Virgil Michel was to transplant successfully to America what had previously been a revival of Roman Catholicism in Europe.

But Virgil Michel's significance extends beyond that. He was one of the few twentieth-century American Catholics to identify the problems of contemporary Christianity as identical with the problems of contemporary secular society. Crises in Church and state were in his eyes the result of a widespread individualism which had permeated the world of worship as well as the world of work. Virgil Michel is remembered today as one of the few American Christians who could bridge the religious and secular spheres in such a way that he could join the call for community in social action to a call for community in the Church. He never isolated his concern "to restore all things in Christ" from "the reduction of man to a mere cog in a machine."[17]

Michel's campaign for the new Catholicism in America evolved in three stages between 1926 and 1938: worship, education, and social justice. From the beginning he understood that a Catholic revival in the United States must be genuinely American to be successful. This meant a broad and practical program embracing as many priests, religious, and members of the laity as could be interested. To begin the mission of a new Catholicism in 1926 an invitation was "extended to all Catholics of whatever rank to cooperate."[18]

In the first stage of this effort in the 1920s, Michel united the talents of a number of liturgists into two institutional projects which became permanent forces for the revival of Catholic worship in the United States—the journal *Orate Fratres* and a publishing house, The Liturgical Press. *Orate Fratres* ("Pray, brethren") made its initial appearance on the first Sunday of Advent in 1926 and within a year had gained two thousand subscribers. Its goal was a restatement of Guéranger's vision in an American context, the "wider spread of the true understanding of and participation in the Church's worship by the general laity in order to foster the corporate life of the natural social units of the Church—the parishes."[19] Like Guéranger, Michel meant to open the well-springs of the liturgy without stirring up the troubled waters of the hierarchy or offending traditional tastes.

The Liturgical Press (its title meant "The People's Work"), also founded in the fall of 1926, pursued similar ideals through its Popular Liturgical Library: to bring lay people back to active participation in the official worship of the Church and thereby make parishes into model communities. Almost all of the initial books published by The Press were by European Catholics, many translated by Father Virgil himself. In 1927 the Popular Liturgical Library included in its list for the first time *Our Mass*, the ordinary of the Mass arranged for the participation of American congregations. This booklet quickly sold 2,500,000 copies.

All of the liturgical work and writings of Virgil Michel had one aim: to make every Catholic keenly aware that he or she must be an apostle in the United States by the very fact of membership in the Mystical Body of Christ. Möhler's teaching on the Mystical Body frames all of Virgil Michel's liturgical writing, and Möhler is the theological foundation for the American's renewal of the communal dimension of the Church and its worship. This thought runs like a core through scores of Virgil Michel publications: in the supernatural community of "the Mystical Body of Christ" is to be found the pattern and inspiration for all celebrations of the Eucharist. "The Catholic needs to learn to cooperate with fellow men in the Mystical Body of Christ, and he will then possess a model of all such cooperation."[20]

The new Catholicism presupposed a sufficient number of thoughtful clergy and laity, people with a broad perspective and a sensitivity to values, Christians who had developed a heart with the skill to listen. The good order of the American Church required that there be a reasonable number of educated and articulate laity, of talented people, of people whose thoughts reached out to wider horizons.

Beginning in 1929 a central part of the mission of Virgil Michel began to be the creation of educational programs designed to form articulate laity thoroughly grounded in the wisdom of the Church, laymen and laywomen schooled in philosophy and theology and in modern Catholic literature. His lay education programs, however, were distinguished from all previous American catechesis in that they flowed from the liturgy. Father Virgil dreamed of a renewal of Catholic education in the spirit of the liturgy:

> Many and varied interests meet in the liturgy. The latter is a great mine of the widest cultural life. There are the literary,

musical, artistic, historical, even ethnological and archaeological aspects, all of which are worth fostering, and all of which are replete with interest and value in life.[21]

In the last years of his life, 1935–1938, Virgil Michel began the third stage of his campaign for the new Catholicism, the outline of programs to effect a Christian social order in the United States. He emphasized directly the social justice implications of the communal Catholicism. This led to practical initiatives at Collegeville as well; for example, the Institute for Social Study designed to train lay leaders in the implementation of Catholic social principles in direct action such as the fostering of credit unions and the foundation of cooperatives and rural life associations.

Spurred on by an apostolic vision of society, lay leaders in Michel's Institute were taught that Christians could gradually reform social institutions by living communally a renewed spiritual life whose source was the liturgy. In this way communal liturgical life could regenerate all of Christian society, and through it, eventually all of American society.

Balancing contemporary politicians and reformers on the left and on the right, Virgil Michel urged United States Catholics neither to escape nor to hide from the dilemmas of Depression America. The choking life of materialism would be transcended only if Christians adopted a system of values whose end was not people but reached beyond men and women and mere concern with the standard of living. The community is formed by that act of reaching beyond. That act is the liturgy. The liturgy expresses the authenticity, austerity, and dignity which overcome the industrial world.

To Virgil Michel the Eucharist is an act which empowers men and women who are right with God to make all earthly things right. By actively participating in worship, American lay Catholics could transform their nation, creating a humane social order which might reflect not just materialism but also the transcendent values of integrity, justice, and beauty.

FOUR INSIGHTS

Virgil Michel lifted before the anxious individuals of his time four insights of the new Catholicism. The first was a renewed sense of the corporate nature of the Church, the idea that the parish is the body that can most effectively carry the Gospel to the world, and that corporate evangelism must have priority of expression in all activities of a congregation and in all the worship of Christians. Through lay participation in the liturgy, congregations could be built up once again into active communities of service and love.

A second insight was that the local Church must be interested in the daily lives of men and women—in their work, in their amusements, and in their social concerns. A parish must be equally interested in and responsibly engaged with national questions, both economic and political, and in the world's problems—hunger and war. Its worship must lay hold of human life and form it not only in the abstract realms of theology but in the concrete realities of marriage, work, sickness, and rest.

A third conviction involved concern for those alienated from the economic order. It was the realization that unemployed industrial workers in Europe felt themselves to be cut off from all hope of lives of fulfillment that led Virgil Michel to see the necessity for new Christian ventures. The unemployed and outcast were the very people whom the Church, if true to Jesus, should be specially searching for. One thing the lonely and poor needed was to feel wanted. One thing that the Church should be able to give was a sense of belonging to a human community. Without community there was no Christian hope for the ragged and the naked, the oppressed and the sweated.

This corporate embrace of others was often lacking and so a fourth emphasis of Virgil Michel was that the foundation of Christian community had to be the renewal of the corporate worship of the laity everywhere. Virgil Michel taught that worship is something that lay persons must do *together* in order to grow into the unity of the Body of Christ. The worship of the Church must express and be seen to express the fullness of the Catholic faith, and it must do so in living, material relation to the life of the people. A liturgy in which all participated would become a witness in America to a new Christian humanism which could safeguard the dignity of the individual within the context of a larger community. Against the gray landscape of the Depression, the breaking of bread could teach in picture language an end to selfishness and narcissism and the emptiness and frustration which result in withdrawal from others.

NOTES

1. Quoted in Steven Lukes, *Individualism* (New York: Harper and Row, 1973) 29.

2. Quoted in Franklin Le Van Baumer, *Readings in Western European Intellectual History from the Middle Ages to the Present* (New York: Alfred A. Knopf, 1967) 455.

3. Quoted in Godfrey Diekmann, *Come, Let Us Worship* (Baltimore: Helicon Press, 1961) 15.

4. Quoted in Peter Nichols, *The Pope's Divisions* (London: Penguin Books, 1981) 294.

5. Quoted in J. M. Shaw, R. W. Franklin, H. Kaasa, *Readings in Christian Humanism* (Minneapolis: Augsburg Publishing House, 1982) 372-73.

6. Michel in Paul Marx, *Virgil Michel and the Liturgical Movement* (Collegeville: The Liturgical Press, 1957) 311. Virgil Michel discusses individualism as the source of these social consequences in *Social Concepts and Problems*, Book One of "The Social Problem" (Collegeville: St. John's Abbey, 1936) 12-19.

7. Karl Marx, *The Communist Manifesto* (New York: Appleton-Century-Crofts, 1955) 12.

8. Karl Marx in Lukes, *Individualism* 71.

9. Rudyard Kipling, *From Sea to Sea*, II (New York: Charles Scribner's Sons, 1913) 230.

10. John Ruskin quoted in E. P. Thompson, *William Morris* (New York: Pantheon Books, 1976) 34.

11. Walter Gropius in *Idee und Aufbau des Staatliches Bauhauses Weimar* quoted in Reyner Banham, *Die Revolution der Architektur* (Hamburg: Rowohlt, 1964) 241-44.

12. Virgil Michel, trans., *A Personalist Manifesto* (New York: Longmans, Green and Co., 1938) xv.

13. Michel, *ibid.* xvi.

14. Letters of J.J.I. Döllinger to E. B. Pusey, February 7, 1842, and May 30, 1866, Pusey House, Oxford; for details on the background of "the new Catholicism," see R. W. Franklin, *Nineteenth Century Churches: The History of New Catholicism in Württemberg, England, and France* (New York and London: Garland Publishing, 1987).

15. J. A. Möhler, "Rezension: F. Walter, *Lehrbuch des Kirchenrechts mit Berücksichtigung der neuesten Verhältnisse,* "*Theologische Quartalschrift* (1823) 294–98; "Rezension: L. Schaaf, *Die Kirchenagenden—Sache in dem preussischen Staate,*" *Theologische Quartalschrift* (1825) 286.

16. *Ecclesiam Suam* of Vatican II, in Peter Foote, *Vatican II's Dogmatic Constitution on the Church* (New York, 1969) 16, 18.

17. Cover of *Orate Fratres* I (November, 1926); Michel, trans, *Manifesto* xvi.

18. Virgil Michel, "Editor's Corner," *Orate Fratres* I (1926) 29.

19. Virgil Michel, "Apostolate, " *Orate Fratres* III (1929) 186.

20. Virgil Michel in Paul Marx, *Virgil Michel* 181.

21. Virgil Michel, "Foreword," *Orate Fratres* I (1926) 2.

3

Virgil Michel: His Life

Today we see more clearly than fifty years ago the central role of Benedictine monasticism in forming the views of Virgil Michel. This is not surprising for he was heir to a monastic tradition that had been devoted to the Christian ideal of community for almost fifteen hundred years and along with this had developed a sense of a special responsibility for the liturgy.

Benedictine monasticism was a way which focused on a self-contained community of people devoted to a life of worship and work in common. In the early sixth century, the *Rule* of St. Benedict laid out a pattern for monasticism that seemed to combine the best of Roman practicality and legality with Christian charity and idealism. The aim of Benedict's *Rule* was simple: to follow the example of Christ as set forth in the Gospels. Benedict's monastery is a renewed Christian society in which Scripture is lived so as to permeate the life of the monk and restructure and reorient the mundane and routine objects and actions of life into a holy vision where God could be truly "all in all."[1]

Reading through the *Rule* today we are struck by how many of its features form the basis of themes restated by Virgil Michel

Virgil Michel in 1916, the year of his ordination.

to United States citizens of the Depression era: the importance attached to worship, the necessity of meaningful labor, the carefully calculated moderation of Christian authority with freedom and diversity, the balance of the needs of the individual monk with the aims of the larger community. Benedict's *Rule* taught the monks the love of a good and Godly world which was to be reshaped through liturgical prayer. In Benedict's vision of a renewed Christian society, work ceased to be regarded as a curse but rather as a gift of God in the service of the human community. Human work tempered by the rhythm of constant worship and nourished by the living waters of the liturgy became a monastic ideal shared by Virgil Michel with his contemporaries who were not monks.

It is also becoming more apparent two decades after Vatican Council II that Benedictine monasticism was central to the rise and growth of the new Catholicism. In many ways the nineteenth-century liturgical movement in Europe, a first stage of the new Catholicism, was also a translation of the Benedictine ideals of worship and work out into the Church at large. Dom Guéranger, the abbot of Solesmes, perceived the necessary institution for a Catholic revival to be the Benedictine monastery, placed as a Christian island fortress in a revolutionary sea. He saw a parallel between his own age and the world of St. Benedict soon after the fall of the Roman Empire, a period of social chaos and barbarism. Benedictine communities had been then and would again be a secure means for the evangelization of secular society.

Though it is to be regretted that the Abbey of Solesmes disengaged one stream of modern monasticism and the Roman Catholic liturgical revival from direct political action toward social change, Benedictine monasteries were at the heart of a modern renewal of Catholic worship and witness around the world. The international character of monasticism allowed monks to carry a program of reform to many nations. The nature of the monastery as an institution which is a center both of learning and of daily life, as well as of prayer, allowed the

Benedictines to absorb other developments in theology and in the social sphere, such as the ecclesiology of Möhler and the great papal encyclicals on social justice which helped to define the new Catholicism.

For example, one stream of Church history links Möhler and Guéranger directly to the Benedictine congregation of Beuron, founded by Dom Maurus Wolter in Germany in 1863. Beuron and three of its daughter houses, Maredsous (1872) and Mont-César (1899) in Belgium and Maria Laach (1892) in the German Rhineland, bore the liturgical movement into the twentieth century and stood behind its explicit recognition by the Vatican in the reign of Pius XI, the first pope to use the term "liturgical movement." From Beuron the liturgical apostolate spread to Benedictine monasteries around the globe, houses that in turn began to touch the laity in increasing numbers.

From 1924 the Beuronese monk who had the greatest influence on Virgil Michel was Lambert Beauduin. Beauduin is another example of how a variety of factors, Guéranger, Möhler, and the papal encyclicals came together within Benedictine monasticism to lead to Catholic action on many fronts. Beauduin's significance lies in the fact that he refashioned previous Benedictine teaching on liturgy and society specifically for a twentieth-century industrial context, and he developed a forward-looking concrete program of teaching and publishing which could actually advance the cause of liturgical evangelization among industrial workers.

THE MONASTIC WORLD

Senator Eugene McCarthy has described the monastic world Virgil Michel stepped into at Collegeville in 1903:

> The monks were still cutting wood on the monastery grounds and hauling it in the wintertime and burning it in their power system generating their own heat and electricity. From this and in many other ways a visitor gained an impression of their ideal of ecological balance, of the earthly paradise and respect for

St. John's Abbey and University in 1907.

the earth and parsimony sustained by the principles of St. Benedict.

Another idea that was very evident in Collegeville was that you ought to try to let every person develop as much as he could. . . .

The idea of competition was not so important. St. John's was marked by the acceptance that you didn't have to compete, that not everyone had to be the same or succeed.[2]

In 1903 St. John's Abbey in Collegeville, Minnesota, was already the largest male community to be established as part of the monastic revival of the nineteenth century. In May 1856 a tiny colony of Bavarian Benedictines had built a priory on the banks of the Mississippi River in St. Cloud. By 1864 the Catholic monks had been forced out of St. Cloud by Protestant Republicans, and they settled on 360 acres of rolling hills and lakes west of the village of St. Joseph, which had just recently been the hunting grounds of the Sioux and the Chippewa. The monks bought the land with 6,000 florins "donated" to them by King Ludwig II of Bavaria. By 1889, 104 monks and 350 students were living and worshiping in the Romanesque revival abbey church and quadrangle the Benedictines had constructed themselves in the Indianbush.

In that year a visiting prelate remarked to the monks, "Your buildings! They are simply gigantic, simply gigantic."[3] The Benedictine monastic community of St. John's had raised in the Minnesota wilderness the largest institutional plant west of the Mississippi. This single huge structure contained within it a monastery, a seminary, a university, and a prep school, all under one roof. In 1894, when a tornado hurled itself against the main St. John's quadrangle, windows were plucked out, chimneys pulled off, shingles pulverized, and the main turret smashed. But the buildings gave not an inch, and when the storm subsided they were there as before, mighty and indomitable.

To some this quadrangle was symbolic of the perseverance of the St. John's community in remaining faithful to its monas-

tic ideals, even when under attack by other elements in the
Catholic Church or in frontier Protestantism. "The Benedic-
tine Order still lives and is destined to thrive even in northern
Minnesota," remarked one pioneer nineteenth-century monk.
"Of course the winds are pretty rough in this far northern re-
gion, storms come and pass away, but the tree planted by St.
Benedict is strong enough to stand the blast."[4]

In one such blast the hard-driving and ambitious second
abbot of St. John's, Alexius Edelbrock, was asked to resign
by Pope Leo XIII in 1889 after the disapproval of neighboring
Irish bishops and some of the original Bavarian members of
his own community made his continued exercise of forceful
leadership impossible. It was soon after the resignation of Abbot Alexius that the influence of the Benedictine liturgical
movement, deriving from Beuron rather than Solesmes, was
first felt at St. John's Abbey in the 1890s under Abbot Bernard Locnikar. For Abbot Bernard the distinctive mission of
the monks on the American frontier was the promotion of liturgical life and the improvement of Church music. Manuals on
worship and Gregorian chant were imported from Beuron to
Minnesota in 1891–1892; the feasts of the Church year began
to be celebrated with much greater liturgical solemnity in the
abbey church, and the Divine Office was accompanied with
Gregorian chant for the first time.

Under Abbot Alcuin Deutsch in the 1920s, the abbey church
at St. John's was redecorated following Beuronese concepts
of liturgical art. The main altar was moved from the apse wall
closer to the middle of the monks' stalls, and representations
of individual saints were replaced by primitive symbols of community as the interior was repainted by Br. Clement Frischauf
of the congregation of Beuron. Today we can still see Brother
Clement's choir of brilliant angels gathering to form a community before the Eucharistic Presence in the Great Hall of
St. John's University.

As a young monk Alcuin Deutsch had spent six years in
Europe absorbing the Benedictine liturgical movement. As ab-

St. John's Abbey Church in 1911.

St. John's Abbey Church in the 1920s after the Beuronese redecoration.

bot of St. John's from 1921, Alcuin Deutsch observed that he had tried to seize this opportunity "to create an interest in the Liturgical Movement. For I have the conviction that a deeper practical understanding and living of the liturgy of the Church is fraught with great possibilities for good to the Christian people and through them to society."[5]

St. John's was therefore a "school" in which Virgil Michel learned four insights about the Christian faith as he progressed, between 1903 and 1924, from status of prep school student to solemnly professed monk and university professor with a Ph.D. These insights were: (1) that God has created human beings as creatures of fellowship; (2) that both matter and spirit are in the service of God's purpose to restore all that belongs to human existence; (3) that in acts of worship we experience what the reign of God can be like; (4) that Christianity bears witness to a humanism which coordinates the material with the spiritual aspects of life in the work of God.

The American boy who was attracted to these ideals was in most respects typical of the urban, prosperous youth growing up in what to our generation appears a golden age of peace and opportunity in the United States. Virgil Michel's father Fred owned a department store in the energetic river town of St. Paul, Minnesota. It was the same time and the same locale in which F. Scott Fitzgerald was coming of age. And there is something of the Great Gatsby about Fred Michel, for having invested $500,000 in opal and silver mines in Mexico, which he subsequently lost in the Mexican Revolution of 1910, and believing himself to be an utter failure, he deserted his family to begin a new life elsewhere.

Yet unlike his contemporary F. Scott Fitzgerald, the young Virgil Michel did not impress others with his gaiety or his brilliance. The boy and the man were marked instead by a singular devotion to duty. "He seemed through his lifetime never to be able to laugh as others do: his [laugh] seemed a very forced one and surely was not attractive either."[6] These are the words of a college classmate who remembered him always with a book: reading while waiting for a partner to arrive for tennis or roaming the St. John's woods on a resplendent spring day with a volume in hand. As a boy he endured one hot St. Paul summer reading all thirty volumes, in German, of the famous writer of Indian stories Karl May; as an undergraduate he wrote a treatise in Latin on Prudentius and translated German patristic texts.

Such a boy in Minnesota during this time had the opportunity to turn to monasticism to further his education. During the early Middle Ages Benedictine monasteries had provided almost the only opportunities for education and learning. Though St. Benedict himself did not leave specific instructions on how monks were to be educated, his contemporary Cassiodorus (480–575) caused a monastery to be founded which quickly became a European center for theological studies. His model of combining monasticism with learning was followed by many later Benedictine monasteries, including St. John's Abbey. Virgil Michel was attracted to St. John's above all as a center of spirituality, learning, and scholarship. Though he joined an abbey in the Indianbush hidden in the woods, he did so in the faith that it possessed a power which could radiate and transform the society of his own time.

From his old novice master Athanasius Meyer, Michel learned that the Benedictine pioneers of the Indianbush in their worship believed that for a moment they beheld paradise already in the landscape around them, even though it was only the barren pine woods of the Midwest. For this reason, they asked the Beuronese artist Br. Clement Frischauf to transport to the entrance of their refectory a portion of the apsidal mosaic of St. John's Lateran in Rome to which earlier Benedictine monks had fled from Monte Cassino. At the door of the monastic dining room in Minnesota, two deer stand atop Calvary converted by the Resurrection into the Mountain of Paradise, while four waterspouts flow from it into the River Jordan. Clearly the monks were suggesting that the monastery named after St. John the Baptist founded in the frontier wilderness was a provisional paradise where novices and students might grow in wisdom and stature by reading from the Book of Nature and from the Book of Scripture.

Through this reading during his early years as a monk, Father Virgil became increasingly concerned about the state of the Catholic Church in his native land. We have used the term "crisis," and it may not be too strong a word to describe the great tensions which then existed between the values of American democracy and those of the Roman hierarchy that the young monk was himself experiencing, along with many of his co-religionists. Encyclicals of Leo XIII and Pius X hurled against "Americanism" had a stultifying effect upon the American Church. Walter J. Ong has written that American Catholics after 1910 "were so chastened . . . that they turned more industriously than ever to developing 'know-how'. . . ."[7]

It is possible to speculate that the tensions inherent in American Catholicism between individualism and hierarchy began to transform Virgil Michel from the bookish youth to the mature man of energy and vision. He himself remarked that feverish study marked his own response to crisis, and he wrote to Abbot Peter Engel in 1918: "I think the best thing for us, especially with the nervous American spirit, is to see ahead of ourselves at all times at least double the work we can manage."[8]

We watch his famous energy begin to emerge and garner achievements: in 1916–1918, a doctorate in English at the Catholic University in Washington; in the summers of 1917–1918 more advanced study at Columbia University with voracious reading at the New York Public Library; in 1919, an early article for the *American Catholic Quarterly Review*. His subject in 1919, as in his Catholic University dissertation, was Orestes Brownson (1803–1876), the self-educated, eccentric spiritual wanderer from Vermont whose journey brought him to Catholicism as the only fulfillment of American ideals.

The commanding personal standard of feverish work was communicated to students grown accustomed to a more relaxed

Bavarian ideal at St. John's, and in the days following World War I Virgil Michel was not popular in Collegeville. As an English teacher he was remembered for the sharpness of his personal comments; as a seminary professor he was said to speak above the level of student comprehension, and as a philosophy instructor he was overheard to launch into nervous discussions of his numerous personal problems and difficulties. He seemed to be passing into adulthood in greater and greater isolation, with study the chief passion of his life.

THE VOICE OF ST. BENEDICT

Then in the 1920s the message of St. Benedict came back to him with new vigor out of the *Rule,* and Virgil Michel experienced a kind of conversion in which he discovered a resolution of the tension between individualism and hierarchy in the *via media* of the Benedictine ideal of community. In the 1920s Virgil Michel became convinced that the spirit of Benedict spoke to the dilemmas facing the Church as it existed at that moment in the United States. He discussed this discovery in greater detail in a later essay on education:

> The Benedictine spirit is the true Gospel spirit in all its comprehensiveness and in all its perfection. . . . Now the need today is not a return to Renaissance spirituality . . . which already shows many traces of decline, but precisely a return to the primitive type, the true Christian spirit, derived from its primary and indispensable source, as Pius X put it. . . . Benedictines have always been acknowledged to have something of this, and they have it the more, the more true they are to their ideal of life.[9]

As paradoxical as it may seem, Michel believed Benedict provided the answer to the questions American Catholics were asking. From ancient to modern times Benedictine monasticism had expressed in a variety of ways the unique insight that both matter and spirit are in the service of human purposes, had been concerned with how the individual relates to the community, and had acknowledged that faith implies freedom as well as authority. Authority, worship, and work: these were the dilemmas of American Catholics and the Benedictine spirit answered "exactly to what the earnest man of today is seeking":[10]

> Our life is very distinctly not one of external formalism, or of a compliance with rules that is the result of external pressure; but it is rather one of sweet reasonableness, common sense, in which perfection of life is the result of inner conviction above all. . . . In the true Benedictine spirit there is nothing of those characteristics against which the modern mind has been reacting: external formalism, traditionalism, the compliance of compulsion. . . ."[11]

BEAUDUIN A DECISIVE INFLUENCE

It is surprising that it was in Europe and in the relatively brief time-span of February 1924 to August 1925 that this conversion took place. It was in Europe that Virgil Michel forged his first plans for introducing "America" to "Benedict." And it is also clear that the thirty-four-year-old monk used this opportunity to escape from Minnesota and "to dash about."[12]

In Europe he experienced something of the personal transformation which was typical of other American expatriots on the Continent in the 1920s. The Minnesota grind gradually became the urbane monk who relished long evenings of talk punctuated with cigars and bourbon. In faded photographs we see him today smiling from the top of a camel before the pyramids, and then fashionably dressed inside an "elite" tour bus on the streets of Berlin. And there are his postcards written in old Jazz Age English reporting sailing "along the whole French, Belgian, and most of Dutch coast," flying in a bi-plane over the English Channel to Amsterdam, hearing Mass at the Vatican: "Reading of the homily lessons a veritable howl-response still worse" (June 13, 1924), rummaging through Jerusalem: "saw some real relics of nail, spikes, parts of real cross. . . .

Virgil Michel, seated in the second row, in a German tour bus in 1924.

believed myself for once undoubtedly in the presence of something big and real" (April 5, 1924).¹³

Father Virgil summed up the purpose of his European sojourn in his own words, "I'm after Benedictine life, churches, and shrines, and the ordinary people. . . ."¹⁴ He recorded his first continental encounter, at the Belgian monastery of Mont-César on February 26, 1924, "Great conversation on needs of American and Benedictine work."¹⁵ Mid-way through his tour he reported back to St. John's, "Since June I have been in fourteen Benedictine monasteries and shall see about ten more in the next months. . . . I learned much."¹⁶ At Maria Laach he studied liturgy, at Beuron art, at Solesmes music, at Maredsous publishing, but it was primarily from Dom Lambert Beauduin of Mont-César that he gained the most significant insights into how a modern monk might make an impact on the contemporary Church and the industrial social order.

Soon after his arrival in Rome, Father Virgil met Dom Lambert who was professor of fundamental theology at the Benedictine College from 1921 to 1925, and Dom Lambert remembered his first impressions of the young American years later:

> I knew him well at Rome and when he discovered that I was concerned with the liturgical movement . . . we became quite friendly, and he often came to talk to me in private. . . . liturgy was not for him just a matter of study; it was above all a powerful means of doing apostolic work, by increasing the faith and devotion of the faithful."[17]

A monk of St. John's rendered this judgment on Beauduin's influence: "All of Dom Lambert's interests became Father Virgil's interests. Beauduin immediately and directly inspired the beginning of Dom Virgil's liturgical apostolate."[18] He did this in three ways.

First, it was Dom Lambert in Rome and Mont-César who deepened the American's understanding of worship by joining the celebration of the Eucharist to an understanding of the Church as the Mystical Body of Christ. Christ's Incarnation, his sacramental body in the Eucharist, and his Mystical Body, the Church, were blended as parts of the same whole by Beauduin and consequently also became inseparable from now on in Virgil Michel's mind. He beheld the Incarnation of the divine Word released into history and society as the risen Christ bestowed his presence on the community of faith.

Second, this social conception of the Incarnation and the hierarchical-community model of the Church implied in it meant that the doctrine of the Church as the Mystical Body of Christ was (1) "the most efficacious antidote to the poison of the secular spirit" of individualism, and (2) the source of the social or collective understanding of the prayer of the liturgy.[19] Because of the Mystical Body "liturgical piety . . . is the best weapon" for combating the evils of secularism, and therefore worship is the pastoral work par excellence of the Church, rather than a rubrical detail.[20]

Third, Beauduin mastered a style of writing, teaching, and publishing that emphasized clarity and mass communication. This style proved to be appealing to the working-class people who were the vast majority of the Church in Beauduin's native Belgium. Beauduin's *La Vie liturgique* gained 70,000 subscribers. Later when he was organizing his own work in Collegeville, Michel took Beauduin's projects as his inspiration. *La Vie liturgique* became *Orate Fratres*, and the first volume of The Liturgical Press's Popular Liturgical Library was a translation of *La Piété de l'Église*, Beauduin's only book.

MONASTICISM AND EVANGELIZATION

What role did Benedictine monasticism play in Beauduin's synthesis now passed on to America? After Dom Lambert's ordination as a secular priest in the 1890s, he had labored eight years with industrial workers as one of the "Chaplains of Workmen" appointed by the Belgian diocese of Liège to forward the practical application of Pope Leo XIII's great social encyclical *Rerum novarum*, an 1891 milestone of Church history in which the Catholic Church had for the first time expressed sympathy for the new industrial working class. In Liège, Beauduin followed Pope Leo in asserting the right of labor to a living wage and decent working conditions. The "Chaplains of Workmen" believed they had a mandate from the pope to go directly to the laborers and associate with them, a departure from previous pastoral practice. As a worker chaplain Beauduin shared meals, conversations, his rooms, and his free time with the workers, striving to create a Christian ambiance in a factory setting.

At first the young Belgian priest demonstrated great enthusiasm and energy for his labor mission; he inspired the construction of a large block of workers' flats in the diocese of Liège, and he strove to lead the workers to new levels of self-respect through cleaner housing, better clothes, a richer diet, and brighter entertainment. Yet direct experience of the de-

humanizing nature of factory work, the long hours of mechanical repetition in dark rooms with bitter toil, left Beauduin
increasingly depressed. The poverty-stricken and those spiritu-
ally and morally enervated stood before him, and he grasped
for a sound basis for rechanneling Christian energies toward
a reconstruction of social relationships.

In the factory world Beauduin came to the conclusion that
the old individual interpretation of Christian ethics had become irrelevant in the face of the brutal facts of daily life. His
little moral homilies and his new houses did not change human
conditions or actions or attitudes in any problem of collective
behavior. Beauduin sought to reestablish a social perspective
on Christian ethics, but what would be its basis? There was
need for a deeper conversion, but what would be its source?

As a secular priest Beauduin perceived that additional spiritual resources were necessary for a program of Christian social action. In 1906 he entered the Benedictine abbey of
Mont-César and there he was brought into contact with fourteen centuries of monastic living with its stress on the liturgy
as the center, not the periphery, of the Christian life. To the
Benedictines, Jesus had sanctioned ceaseless prayers of praise,
blessing, and thanksgiving, and if there were no active community of worship in which all participated, the monastery
would have no reason for existing.

THE BENEDICTINE INFLUENCE

It was because of the stress on the active participation of all
at Mont-César that Dom Lambert remarked that he learned
from the monks for the first time the real meaning of the Eucharist, that it is the offering of the whole community and that
for this reason the communitarium character of the Church
is above all made manifest in the Eucharist. A communal Eucharist is the key to other Christian community: "It is in the
celebration of the Mass that the body of assembled Christians
intensifies its life as the mystical Body of Christ from the Eucharistic Body."[21]

Yet coming as he did from a previous slum ministry, Dom Lambert quickly perceived that this monastic model was precisely what the factory parishes required. If lay Catholics could be brought by active participation in the Eucharistic liturgy to think of themselves as a community, they would soon have an answer to the social question, which was at its root an issue of individualism and alienation. If liturgical worship were restored as the corporate action of the whole Christian people, including the laity, it would be able to lift society from the miserable conditions created by the industrial revolution. Beauduin demanded that the Catholic Church not hide from the contemporary industrial world of machine work but meet it and transform it through the people's work, the liturgy, so that the world of the sacraments, the world into which the liturgy introduces us, could bring the new life of the Resurrection into the sphere of factories, machines, shops, and strikes.

Dom Lambert surpassed all of his predecessors in creating the right media to disseminate this message to the secular clergy and their parishioners. In this he essentially adapted the unique resources of a monastery to the needs of the liturgical apostolate in the parish. The emphasis here was on the parish, the institution understood by Beauduin as the key to the spiritual revival of the whole Church. Weekly inexpensive liturgical guides, reviews, and pamphlets were issued by Beauduin with the help of confreres at Mont-César. In 1909 *La Vie liturgique*, a weekly paper, began to be distributed in Belgium, and in 1910 it was carried into Holland. In that year *Questions liturgiques et paroissiales*, a quarterly, was begun in order to defend the liturgical movement in the theological language of the day. The faithful received books edited by a staff of monks in the *Petite bibliotheque liturgique* series after 1912. The whole monastery was mobilized for these endeavors, even to the point of shifting class schedules so that publication deadlines might be met. The resources of the monastery were shared with secular clergy: library, church, refectory, for the purpose of awakening the liturgical apostolate in annual Liturgical Weeks conducted at Mont-César. Two hundred and fifty secular priests came in 1910, and one of these left this account of his "conversion" to a new vision of Christianity:

> These days will be remembered among the best of my life. New horizons have been opened to me; the Missal, the Breviary, the Ritual . . . what a revelation, and after thirty-seven years of priestly life! . . . Until this time my piety has been individualistic, exclusive, Protestant. From now on it will be collective, social, and Catholic.[22]

The success of these endeavors dazzled Father Virgil; the teaching of Dom Lambert led to his own spiritual renewal. He became convinced that a similar popular liturgical movement was the great need for the revival of the Roman Catholic Church in America. More and more Virgil Michel began to copy Beauduin's personal style. The Belgian's biographer tells us that he often worked through the night, kept awake by a pot of hot black coffee brought to him by one of his brother monks. His articles composed in the haste of the moment appear to be more recorded conversations than carefully wrought prose. And in a similar manner Michel was prepared to harness the energies of St. John's Abbey to the goal of a liturgical awakening as Beauduin had done with those of Mont-César. "Just think," he wrote Abbot Alcuin during his last months in Europe, "how it would help to transform the mentality towards the liturgy at home, not to think of the possible providential work that lies before us in the whole English-speaking world."[23] The American liturgical movement would be the first step toward a new Catholicism in the United States.

THE AMERICAN LITURGICAL MOVEMENT

The historic mission of Virgil Michel was now to transplant successfully to America what had previously been essentially a Belgian, French, and German development. In 1926 Michel organized the two projects which became permanent forces for the revival of worship in America: the journal *Orate Fratres*

Virgil Michel's permission to live in Belgium for four months in 1924–1925. His signature appears on the lower left-hand corner of the document.

and The Liturgical Press. Within only three years *Orate Fratres* was appearing in twenty-six countries, and Michel's dream was quickly fulfilled: *Orate Fratres* had become the official voice of the liturgical movement to the English-speaking Catholic world.

But this success was not achieved without a costly personal price. The man was driven to ever increasing amounts of work by the vision he had gained in Europe. He wrote more than a third of the first number of *Orate Fratres* himself as well as the first three translations of the Popular Liturgical Library. He was director of The Liturgical Press, its financial custodian, and the author of a stream of leaflets, brochures, and circulars on the liturgical apostolate which poured out of Collegeville until 1930. The vast labor of organizing a staff of associate editors for *Orate Fratres* and coordinating collaborators for The Liturgical Press all fell on his shoulders. And there was the avalanche of letters to write which consumed him, articles to commission or reject, reviewers to solicit, and critics to mollify, from morticians disturbed at his new emphasis on simple funerals to bishops who banned *Orate Fratres* from their seminaries. To Irish bishops on the East and West Coasts, Michel's American liturgical works were merely "a meeting of a bunch of Germans out in the Midwest."[24] Another typical critic was Sr. Antonia McHugh, President of the College of St. Catherine in St. Paul, who wrote:

> The liturgical movement centered at St. John's, which aims to diffuse social charity and understanding through increased lay participation in the official worship of the Church, is something with which I will have nothing to do. The thought of connecting the psalms with socially activated prayers is too irritating to be considered. The whole commotion is doubtless of German origin.[25]

The attempt to hold together the tensions of worship in his monastery with work in the liturgical apostolate and the strain inherent in launching a movement for community within a hierarchical Church proved to be too much, and in the summer of 1930 Virgil Michel suffered a severe breakdown. His "indomitable will had worn out both eyes and nerves."[26] He had to be confined to a dark hospital room. Through the summer of 1930 he was assaulted by severe headaches and could find neither rest nor sleep. Released from liturgical obligations, he was sent to the Siberia of northern Minnesota for almost three years, there to engage in mild forms of missionary endeavor.

We are not surprised to learn that upon arriving at Cass Lake in the north country in 1930 and at the White Earth missions in 1931 "he embraced with zeal" the culture of the native Americans.[27] Among the Indians he experienced a kind of second conversion, a renewed Roman Catholic commitment to the priesthood of every Christian, an idea which contained within it revolutionary implications.

NOTES

1. *Holy Rule*, chapter 72.

2. Eugene J. McCarthy, MS Reflections on Saint John's Abbey in the Early Twentieth Century (1982) 27–28, Archives, St. John's Abbey, Collegeville, Minnesota.

3. Archbishop John Ireland in 1888 quoted in Colman J. Barry, *Worship and Work* (Collegeville: St. John's Abbey, 1956) 154.

4. Letter of Alexius Edelbrock, June 27, 1878, Archives, Convent of St. Benedict, St. Joseph, Minnesota.

5. Alcuin Deutsch, "The Liturgical Movement," *Emmanuel* 32 (August, 1926) 239.

ɔ. Letter of Sylvester Harter, March 8, 1953, Archives, St. John's Abbey, Collegeville, Minnesota.

7. Walter J. Ong, *Frontiers in American Catholicism: Essays on Ideology and Culture* (New York: The Macmillan Company, 1957) 21–22.

8. Letter of Virgil Michel, March 3, 1918, Archives, St. John's Abbey, Collegeville, Minnesota.

9. Virgil Michel, "The Basic Need of Christian Education Today," *The Proceedings of the National Benedictine Educational Association* XII (1929) 41–42.

10. *Idem.*

11. *Idem.*

12. Virgil Michel diary, May 30, 1925, Archives, St. John's Abbey, Collegeville, Minnesota.

13. Virgil Michel diary, May 30, 1925, June 13, 1924, April 5, 1924, Archives, St. John's Abbey, Collegeville, Minnesota.

14. Letter of Virgil Michel, April 20, 1924, Archives, St. John's Abbey, Collegeville, Minnesota.

15. Virgil Michel diary, February 26, 1924, Archives, St. John's Abbey, Collegeville, Minnesota.

16. Letter of Virgil Michel, September 10, 1924, Archives, St. John's Abbey, Collegeville, Minnesota.

17. Letter of Lambert Beauduin, September 26, 1952, Archives, St. John's Abbey, Collegeville, Minnesota.

18. Paul Marx quoted in his *Virgil Michel and the Liturgical Movement* (Collegeville: The Liturgical Press, 1957) 28; Jeremy Hall in her *The Full Stature of Christ* (Collegeville: The Liturgical Press, 1976) 12.

19. Lambert Beauduin, *Liturgy: The Life of the Church*, trans. by Virgil Michel (Collegeville: The Liturgical Press, 1929) 28.

20. Beauduin, *ibid.* 31.

21. Jeremy Hall, *The Full Stature of Christ* 13.

22. *Questions liturgiques et paroissiales* I (1911) 439.

23. Letter of Virgil Michel, January 18, 1925, Archives, St. John's Abbey, Collegeville, Minnesota.

24. J. J. Murphy, "A Call for Irish-American Honest Self-Appraisal," *The Homiletic and Pastoral Review* LIV (March, 1954) 509–13.

25. Helen Angela Hurley, *On Good Ground* (Minneapolis: University of Minnesota Press, 1951) 261.

26. Paul Marx, *Virgil Michel* 161.

27. Paul Marx, *ibid.* 163.

4

The People's Worship

"We the people" today is a much cherished phrase on the lips of all Americans who reflect on the past two centuries of their Constitution. The liberation of "the people" from monarchs who held supreme power is the central political event of modern history, and it came when the masses grew restive under a situation in which decisions concerning their lives were made by those above them. All the freedoms won by the democratic revolutions that we hold dear—the right to free speech, the right to free assembly, the right to freedom of conscience, the very rights to work, to travel, and to pursue happiness—these made ordinary citizens for the first time fully active participants in the creation of their own destinies.

The liturgical movement in Europe, and even more in America, cannot be separated from this historical setting. The liberation of "the people" from centuries of passivity at worship was part of the spirit of the times. The prism of life was shifting dramatically to the role of the masses in processes of social change, in the transformation of institutions, and in the evolution of society in all its marvelous complication and rich variety.

In a parallel manner, the liturgical movement strove to enfranchise the laity at worship through education, so that the

VOLUME I   NOVEMBER 28, 1926   NUMBER 1

ORATE·FRATRES

INSTAVRARE
OMNIA·IN·CHRISTO

The initial number of *Orate Fratres* of November 28, 1926, with Eric Gill's design portraying the heavenly city Jerusalem with the motto below "To reestablish all things in Christ."

Mass would become a comprehending act to the masses. It sought to give ordinary lay Catholics a voice through the encouragement of the active participation of all in the singing, responses, processions, and reception of Communion at each celebration of the Eucharist. To Virgil Michel the principal goal of the American liturgical revival, as regards the laity, was to "restore to them their native right to a share in . . . knowledge and understanding. . . ."[1] The very first issue of *Orate Fratres* in 1926 stated that liturgical renewal above all "must come through a sympathetic understanding on the part of the general faithful"; and Michel restated the reason for the restoration of American Catholic worship again in 1930: "Our aim and the need among us is first of all to reestablish the proper union" between laity and clergy.[2]

The extent of the impact of the revival of the role of the laity in the United States associated with the name Virgil Michel makes a descriptive term for his work difficult. Here and there it has been called a "restoration," a "revival," and a "renewal," but those words miss the connotation of an American movement evolving along a creative "middle way" which was at once conservative, in that it looked to the Benedictine past for models, and progressive, in that it sought to create a revived community life appropriate for modern conditions through worship.

From the perspective of the long story of the waxing and waning of the ideal of the human community as reflected in the history of liturgy, now for almost two thousand years, of the changing shape of "the people" at a liturgy from community to hierarchy, of the acquiescence of "the people" before priestly elites, of their subordination through the rise and the fall of a pervasive Christian individualism—from this perspective perhaps "reformation" is the right word to describe the liturgical movement. Perhaps a second reformation did begin among the Benedictines. That word does convey the idea that this was a religious change that was not confined to one continent, that it was a movement occurring in a succession of monastic centers. However, the change wrought by the liturgical movement in America was slower, less dramatic, more diffuse and illusive than the sixteenth-century events that go by the name Reformation.

HISTORY OF LITURGY

Sometimes the transformation in the meaning of a word such as liturgy comes closer to the bedrock of history than what we conventionally call events and illustrates best the monumental, though subtle, shift in the place of the laity in the Church wrought by reforms of the sort advocated by Virgil Michel. Liturgy fulfills this function in an exceptional manner because it is a word of great interest, one which has acquired a deeper resonance as it has described each successive stage of the place of the laity in Christian worship. By the fifth century B.C. in Athens, the Greek terms for people and for work came to be fused into the word *leitourgia*, to designate public tasks performed by the free populace of the ancient polis. Liturgy meant "the people's work."

The Alexandrian translators of the Septuagint first used the word liturgy to describe the Hebrew worship of God in the third century B.C. *Leitourgia* appears 127 times in the Septuagint, and there it means the public work of the sacred cult performed in homage to God by priests and levites juridically invested and set above the masses. The prayers of the assembly of the laity gathered in the court of the Israelites or in the Women's Court in the Temple of Jerusalem are not defined as liturgy.

A significant departure from Septuagint usage occurs in the New Testament at Acts 13:1-2 where the New Testament writer employs *leitourgia* in a manner closer to its original classical Greek sense: an action performed by an entire human community rather than by a hierarchy. The verse points to a revolutionary turn away from a cultic priesthood and a lack of emphasis on persons of rank that were characteristic of the early Christian Church. Acts 13:2 glances back five hundred years to the ancient image of the great corporate liturgies of the assembly of the free citizens of the polis to describe the worship of Jesus Christ, in which each Christian took an equal share, as a liturgy.

The Apostle Paul used the Greek word *koinonia* (in Latin *communio*, hence the Protestant English word "Communion" for liturgy) to describe the fellowship, sharing and mutual affection which were essential ingredients of the worship of the early Christians.

At the heart of Christian worship was the sharing of a meal of bread and wine, a universal emblem of community throughout the culture of humankind. Though documentation is scarce, a case can be made that the Christian Eucharist may rightly be classed as the people's work until the late fourth century, in the sense that all members of the community, including the laity, took an active part in the reading, singing, processing, and preaching that together made up the liturgy. The laity maintained an active participation in the ministry of the Word, individual believers freely stepping forward from the assembly to read at the Eucharist, until the distinct office of "lector" emerged in the third century.

Among the first great theologians, Justin, Tertullian, and Clement of Alexandria were teachers not ordained. While still a learned layman with his own school of Scripture, Origen was invited to preach before the bishops of Caesarea and Jerusalem in the first half of the third century. However, in most places in the course of the third century, it became normal that preaching at liturgical services was usually confined to the clergy, with presbyters and bishops continuing to share together in the ministry of the Word, retaining this one element of its primitive corporate nature when preaching had been open to anyone who displayed appropriate talents.

Even in the third century, an individual lay person at the liturgy may still have recited the Eucharistic prayer over the bread and the wine *ex tempore*, but this practice did not last and evidence indicates that by the beginning of the fourth century the Eucharistic prayer became an exclusively clerical activity. Yet into the fifth century the assembly still cried out its assent to the president's blessing of the bread and of the wine by shouting, "Amen!—so be it."

The Eucharistic prayer stood between an offertory procession and a Communion procession which were both all-inclusive. A mosaic survives at Aquileia in Italy from the fourth-century era of the Roman emperor Constantine that represents an offertory procession in which lay women and lay men are bringing bread and wine, grapes, flowers, and birds to the altar. It was general practice that each man and woman should place upon the altar a little loaf of bread and a small bottle of wine, representing the offering of self.

The liturgy ended with all present consuming the bread and the wine while standing before the altar. A precious gospel book from Rossano in Southern Italy of around A.D. 500 pictures Jesus standing while giving his disciples, standing with him, Communion from one loaf of bread. To eat and drink standing before the altar was the final sign of the equality and dignity of all who participated in this "people's work" shaped by anonymous generations of every class out of the common experiences, the culture, and the living language of the laity and possessed of elementary forms familiar to all. The stones and the furniture for the gathering-place for worship, the clothes and the vessels for the celebration, the tithes and the oblations for the offertory were all taken from the ordinary world of the people and possessed of a great simplicity.

DECLINE OF LAY PARTICIPATION

And yet from the time of the late Roman Empire, certainly by the end of the fourth century A.D., Christian liturgy slipped quietly into new modes of celebration which could not be defined as "the people's work," in the sense of a communal action at which the laity were equal participants with the clergy. From the Italian peninsula to the British Isles, worship disappeared as the act of the royal, priestly people of God on pilgrimage as through time it became a highly clericalized function with all action, speaking, and prayers performed by ordained persons, bishops, presbyters, and deacons. As the whole Western Church slowly shifted to accepting the radically new position of bishop and presbyter as "celebrant" of the rite, a growing number of manifestations revealed that Christian liturgy was now as sharply divided by ecclesiastical, hierarchical class as the worship sanctioned by the Hebrew Bible had been.

The celebrant began to turn his back to the congregation, and to recite the prayer of consecration over the bread and the wine in such a way that the eyes of the laity were no longer directed to the oblation. The Western Church conceived of the Eucharistic prayer in the Middle Ages as a sanctuary shut off to all but the ordained, like the Hêkal or Holy of Holies of the Temple at Jerusalem. While the Christian church evolved from the fourth-century Constantinian basilica to the Gothic cathedral of the twelfth century, the unobstructed space and the undifferentiated hall characteristic of the setting for the primitive liturgy were lost amid physical barriers set up to mark out separate spaces where only the clergy might enter to offer worship, spaces reminiscent of the courts in the Jerusalem Temple which divided the place of the cultic work of the priests from the assembly of Israel.

As Christian worship ceased to be "the people's work" in the Church in the West, *leitourgia* came to be used once again by Western Christians in the sense of the Septuagint. For example, in the decrees of the Council of Ancirano of 314 and of the Council of Antioch of 341 or in the *Apostolic Constitutions* of 400, liturgy designates only the prayers of ordained persons in public worship, not the prayers of the laity. The Western fathers Ambrose and Augustine in the fourth century begin to translate *leitourgia* into Latin as *ministerium* and they invest the clergy alone with the power to lead public liturgical prayer.

The people of God became a silent, stationary mass, watching the clergy, kneeling while the bishop or priest stood, declining more and more to eat the consecrated bread, abstaining from the cup after the thirteenth century. By the year 1000 in the minds of most theologians the people's participation had little or nothing to do any longer with the praise and thanksgiving of the Eucharistic offering, and for the next five hundred years it was easy for pastoral practice to dictate that worship was a way of piety for the individual soul and for artistic representations of the Eucharist to contain an individual, psychological emphasis that evoked less a common meal, the most famous example being Leonardo Da Vinci's painting of the disciples asking at the Last Supper, "Lord, is it I?"

Leitourgia fell into disuse and almost completely disappeared as a word used to describe an entire Western Christian service of Eucharistic worship. After the fifth century the adjective *liturgicus* was not commonly used until it was given currency again by sixteenth-century humanist scholars under the influence of the Renaissance rediscovery of Greek texts. "Liturgy" was finally brought back into popularity among Catholic scholars to define a whole service of the Eucharist by two famous and influential publications of the seventeenth century, the Italian Cardinal Bona's *Rerum liturgicarum libri duo* (1671) and the French Benedictine Jean Mabillon's *De liturgia gallicana libri tres* (1685). But the word was not generally used again before the nineteenth century, and it is scarcely to be found in the official acts of any Western Churches before the twentieth.

MICHEL'S DEFINITION OF LITURGY

It has been necessary to give this brief history of the evolution of the definition of liturgy, for only in this way can we appreciate fully the radical departure from the traditional status of the laity implied in the choice of the phrase "liturgical move-ment" for the Benedictine revival of worship and the historic shift that occurred in 1926 when Virgil Michel decided to name the principal organs of his American movement The Liturgical Press and *Orate Fratres*. These words speak of a revolutionary call for a return to the earliest structures of Christian worship with their unfamiliar participatory roles for lay persons.

In his translations for The Liturgical Press and in articles for *Orate Fratres*, Virgil Michel stated explicitly that "the people" or the *laos* at worship are not an audience but a community. In stressing that the liturgy of the Church must be permeated from the beginning to the end by the ideal of community, the American Benedictine fixed on lay participation as the supreme key to renewal, without which there could be no Catholic reemphasis on the experience of fellowship in worship. No one could reinforce a consciousness of Christian solidarity in the twentieth century without an active laity.

While Michel sought for the assembly as a whole a priestly role in the liturgy and he wished to awaken the laity once again to the priestly dimension of their calling, this "universal priesthood" which he stressed by no means precluded some other particular limbs of the Body of Christ from having special and unique leadership functions in the celebration of the Eucharist. Michel held that within the Catholic Church there must continue to be a variety of charisms, services, tasks, and roles. It was clear to him that not all Christians are leaders but only some have been given this charism. Bishops in the apostolic succession and ordained priests are absolutely essential limbs of the Body of Christ to this loyal son of the Church. Their presence and presidency for him enshrined Catholic principles of discipline and unity without which worship could not be valid. Michel maintained that lay persons form an entirely separate class cut off from the government of the Church. He advanced the image of the bishops as the historic focus, though by no means the exhaustive repository, of oversight, authority, and unity within the Christian community.

Yet lay inferiority was an unacceptable form of argument to him based on a sinful human emulation of secular institutions and specifically condemned by Paul in 1 Corinthians 12:14-21. The responsibilities of the ordained are not manifestations of individual or isolated powers which they alone possess. They are symbolic representations of the unified Body of Christ. For example, what is accomplished at the altar is by no means something done to or for a congregation by the bishop or the ordained priest: it is done by God through the whole body of the Church. Of the many biblical images of the people of God as community, the figure of the Body of Christ gives the best clues to Virgil Michel's understanding of the relationship between the participation of everyone present at a liturgy, the ordained with the laity, and the experience of Christian community. He was fond of quoting Paul on this point: "When we break the bread, is it not a means of sharing in the body of Christ . . . God has so adjusted the body, giving the greater honor to the inferior part, that there may be no discord in the body. . . ."[3]

Michel returned constantly to the earliest definition of liturgy as "the people's work" to justify placing the laity at the heart of the liturgical revival in America. The word liturgy and the phrase "people's work" became almost proof-texts in his lexicon to illustrate the basic truth that Christianity is a shared faith that must no longer be understood as the preserve of any one group or class within the Church. For example, in 1929 he said that "the people's work" means the laity "*do the Mass along with the priest,*" and in 1927 liturgy is defined as "above all corporate activity, a fellowship in action. . . . [During the liturgy] some share in the priestly character must be possessed by all the faithful."[4] He provided the fullest definition of liturgy, relating the meaning of the word explicitly to lay participation in worship, in his volume *The Liturgy of the Church*, published in 1937. Here liturgy is

the way to salvation and sanctification for all mankind. . . . Participation in the liturgy naturally produces in us the consciousness of our union with Christ and of our dignity as sharers in the divine nature. . . . [Participation gives us] a better sense of unity with and sympathy for our fellow members of the body of Christ, a human family feeling for all mankind. . . . [It is] the new life; continual growth of this new life in the communion of saints by drinking deeply from the primary and indispensable source—[that] is the liturgy![5]

This single-minded devotion to the laity sprang from one of the paradoxes of Michel's complex personality. He was a monk who was often isolated and personally driven by his own iron will to excesses of labor within the confines of St. John's Abbey. He could be severe and forbidding in his relations with other ordained Benedictines, aloof with brothers and clerics, and frequently absent from monastic prayers. And yet he was completely at home among the laity: affable, warm-hearted, filled with good cheer, ready to talk, eat and drink, and even entertain noisy children.

LAY LEADERS AND GOALS

No Roman Catholic priest in North America so consistently and strongly called for an active Catholic laity as Virgil Michel. From 1926 to 1930 he extended an invitation to co-discipleship through *Orate Fratres* "to all Catholics of whatever rank, to cooperate in the liturgical apostolate by whatever means lay within the possibility of the individuals."[6] In an early editorial for *Orate Fratres* he remarked that, though there were a surprising number of lay readers and subscribers to the magazine, most lay persons hesitated to send him articles or to express themselves regarding the liturgy, as if it were the preserve of the ordained alone. One reader had ended a page of liturgical commentary with "Of course, I am only a layman." Father Virgil wrote back: " 'Only a layman!' We are tempted to answer: 'For such is the kingdom of heaven.' "[7]

Of the original board of associate editors of *Orate Fratres*, two were representatives of the lay order. One was a lay

woman, Justine Ward, a wealthy American disciple of Dom
Guéranger and a Gregorian chant expert in her own right. She
accepted Michel's invitation to join the board at once with a
note from Solesmes: "All that you write of the awakening of
interest in the Liturgy in America . . . fills me with joy."[8]

However, the most influential lay person on the *Orate
Fratres* board was Donald Attwater of England. Michel once
remarked that Attwater was his ideal of what a Catholic lay
person could become in the twentieth century. He was editor
of Caldey Abbey's *Pax* and *Notes for the Month*, both organized attempts in England to spread knowledge of the liturgy among the people; he was well known in British artistic
and theological circles, and he was often sought out for advice by bishops. The quality of *Orate Fratres* was undoubtedly
improved by the keen observations of Attwater who relayed
to Michel the barbed criticisms of British Catholics. It was
characteristic of Father Virgil that he received lay rejoinders
with an easy grace, while his relationships with clergy could
be prickly.

Attwater did much to insure that *Orate Fratres* would be
pleasing in appearance. He enlisted the English lay artist Eric
Gill to design covers for the first volumes of the magazine.
The initial number of November 28, 1926 bore Gill's now-
famous design portraying the heavenly city Jerusalem with a
slain lamb dominating it and the motto below "to reestablish
all things in Christ."

Though an enlightened and zealous laity was a principal
element of the Church "to reestablish," Michel cautioned a
"slow, peaceful evolution" toward this goal from 1926 to 1930.[9]
He was thoroughly a Benedictine in initially advocating such
a pace, and in other ways the first four years of the liturgical
movement in this country were dominated by Benedictine
values. Michel saw the liturgy, long the source of the Benedictine spirit, now amid the conditions of paganism and materialism of the Roaring Twenties, to be the necessary and
neglected resource also of the spirituality of all Christians. This

commitment to the laity was rooted likewise in the origins of Benedictine monasticism as a lay movement.

In addition, Michel adapted three traditional skills of the monastery—reproducing texts, scholarship, and teaching—to his endeavor of popularizing the liturgy. A widespread sharing of the unique resources of the Benedictines would allow the liturgy once again to become the teacher of the people and move the laity from a facade Catholicism to a genuine Catholicism. The American Benedictine had three goals in providing for the dissemination of monastic materials to the population at large: (1) to diminish the separation of the Eucharist from daily affairs; (2) to transform the piety of the laity; (3) to establish stronger bonds between the clergy and their congregations.

At the same time, there was something genuinely American about this movement from 1926 to 1930. It was marked strongly by a conviction that education was the primary means to the liberation of the laity and that mass communication was a legitimate medium for the instruction of the Catholic public. *Orate Fratres*, its forty-eight pages sent out monthly from St. John's Abbey to three thousand subscribers by 1930, was dedicated first to an increase in knowledge and understanding so that the laity could enter more fully into the spirit of worship. Abbot Alcuin Deutsch of St. John's cautioned Father Virgil that a thorough liturgical catechesis was the necessary prelude to any revival of the primitive roles of the laity in worship, such as reading, processing, or vernacular Masses. Abbot Alcuin reminded Father Virgil that ". . . unless you teach the people to penetrate into its inner spirit, you are merely getting the people to substitute one form of prayer for another."[10] In order to restore the laity to their rightful place it was necessary, according to the abbot, "to lead them gradually into a deeper meditative understanding of its text and spirit."[11] He was concerned that active participation not be perceived as a new Catholic fad, a gimmick to entice people into church, but rather as a renewal of the ancient function of the

Eucharistic assembly which alone explains the traditional structure of the Mass.

LITURGY AND EDUCATION

Abbot Alcuin's words summarize exactly the contents of the articles and editorials Virgil Michel wrote for *Orate Fratres* which sought to provide information to allow the laity to unite in heart and mind in the closest possible manner with everything that is said and done by the priest at the altar. Michel developed six themes—piety, dogma, ritual, calendar, sources, and music—to advance the entrance of the laity into the action of the Mass.

1. Lay Piety Becomes Liturgical

At a time when the prayer-life of most American Roman Catholics focused on such devotions as the Rosary, Michel sought a marked change in public attitudes in which the liturgy would displace the Rosary as the chief object of religious experience. He wanted the laity to see the immense superiority of liturgical prayer over private, subjective devotions—the best way to pray is to use the official prayers of the Church. In the words of a German observer, the pages of *Orate Fratres* revealed the liturgy as "the best teacher of the *via ordinaria*— the regulation of religious life in common, with, at the same time, a view to actual needs and requirements. . . ."[12] Each issue of *Orate Fratres* contained a section entitled "The Apostolate" which went beyond anything in European Benedictine reviews in proposing practical lay projects in liturgical living, in keeping readers informed of lay liturgical activities the world over, and in outlining topics of discussion for the hundreds of study clubs which had sprung up to foster entry into a liturgical consciousness through personal experience.

2. The Dogmatic Teaching of the Liturgy

A second major task of *Orate Fratres* in its early years was
to formulate and clarify in precise language the doctrinal teaching of the prayers of the liturgy. The austere restraint and symbolic imagery of liturgical language was unfamiliar to many,
and Michel explained the theological underpinnings of the
prayer formulae and how they spoke of the redemption
wrought in Jesus Christ. Another thrust of Michel's early writings was to relate liturgical doctrine to concrete human experiences.

3. The Meaning of Ritual

A third message was that Americans should not investigate
Christianity chiefly by determining what Catholic theologians
say in their books but by what the Church does in the liturgy.
Orate Fratres unlocked the fundamental catechesis contained
within the gestures, postures, and material objects used in the
Mass. The hope was that a feeling for symbolism would be
awakened in the Catholic public and that concrete signs would
become once again vehicles for the expression of spiritual
reality.

4. Explanation of the Liturgical Year

A fourth series of articles unfolded the riches and the gran-
deur of the liturgical year. The laity were provided information so that they could follow the life of Christ as it was
presented in its various aspects through the liturgical calendar. Michel wished worship to reinforce a consciousness of
solidarity not only with the living but with witnesses to Jesus
Christ who have come before us. He wanted to make the people
aware of a human chain that reached back to the apostles. To
do this, he explained in detail saints' days. The commemora-
tion of saints in the liturgical calendar was seen as another
powerful means for the laity to enter into the Catholic spirit.

5. A Return to the Sources

A fresh appreciation of Holy Scripture was a key element of the liturgical revival. *Orate Fratres* made the case that intelligent congregational participation must be based on a return to the sources: above all the Bible and the Fathers. As editor, Virgil Michel wished his magazine to reorient Christian instruction along the lines of thorough-going biblical knowledge, and in addition to biblical texts he provided his readers with extracts from the sermons and the biblical commentaries of the Fathers as a further means for the general public to enter into a deep and detailed knowledge of the Word of God. The liturgical revival would allow the Bible's message to be seen for what it is: the story of the actions of a loving God to reconcile the whole human family and to redeem the world.

6. A New Spirit in Church Music

In an era when Catholics rarely sang in church, and when they did they preferred patriotic songs or hymns like "Mother Dear, Oh Pray for Me," Michel strove to make liturgical music appreciated by the masses, and he encouraged lay persons to sing chants and hymns during the celebration of the Eucharist. Congregational singing was one of the essentials of liturgical reform. Virgil Michel understood the power of community singing to weld the members of a group together. He held a vision of a singing Church. He saw that the Christian education of many parishes would come more effectively through a hymnbook and through the chants than through preaching. In a singing congregation Virgil Michel saw the Holy Spirit of God actively nurturing human hearts.

RESOURCES FOR THE LAITY

The Liturgical Press from its inception in 1926 served the laity especially in its pamphlet series "The Popular Liturgical Library." This is a name still used today, and "The Library" supplemented in a practical vein the articles of *Orate Fratres* through the production of parish resources. During the twelve years of Virgil Michel's directorship, "The Popular Liturgical Library" sold seven hundred thousand pamphlets at a cost of ten to thirty-five cents. The two most popular of these made the active participation of the laity a reality for the first time in the history of this country. *Offeramus* (We offer) contained the Latin and English texts of all the prayers of the Holy Eucharist. In addition, *Offeramus* contained instructions so that a congregation could engage in a dialogue with the presiding priest. This dialogue Mass booklet quickly spread across the United States, and nearly 150,000 copies were sold before 1938. It went through twenty-three editions, and in 1929 was even translated into Zulu.

Our Mass was a second best seller containing the ordinary of the Mass arranged for congregational participation. It made its appearance in 1927 and in a few years had sold two and one-half million copies. Ninety thousand copies of pamphlet editions of translations of other sacramental rites—baptism, confirmation, marriage, anointing—were in circulation from The Liturgical Press from 1928 to 1938.

Father Virgil brought out *Why the Mass*, a summary of his *Orate Fratres* teaching, and in quick succession his own translations of Dom Lambert Beauduin's *Liturgy, the Life of the Church* and Abbot Emmanuel Caronti's *The Spirit of the Liturgy*. In order to encourage singing, The Press published *The Parish Kyriale*, a booklet containing the texts and notation of fourteen Gregorian chant Masses arranged for parish congregation. Nearly twenty-five thousand copies were sold in the first six months of publication. The entire booklet was hand-set, note by note, at St. John's Abbey to make it possible to keep the price at ten cents and thus within the reach of the mass of the laity.

COMMUNICATION

It was his ability to communicate in clear and direct language to the laity, along with his great energy and capacity for work, which was Virgil Michel's great strength. It is fair to refer to him at this period as more of a journalist or synthesizer, who read all available literature on a topic by keeping to an exacting schedule throughout the day and then writing, sometimes hastily and through the night, essays from the various sources procured for him by other St. John's monks. "Father Virgil," writes the modern historian of St. John's Abbey Colman Barry, "despite his wide reading and exhaustive study, was not a profound scholar. He produced no original research study based on primary sources in his short and overcrowded life."[13]

Father Colman's assertion is certainly true. There could be a superficial quality to Michel's writing from 1926 to 1930. Today it is easy to criticize the primitive books, pamphlets, and articles of the first years of the liturgical movement for their naiveté, for their subservient attitudes toward author-

Virgil Michel arrives at a northern lake in 1930.

ity, for their lack of theological precision. And yet these pioneering attempts inspire us by their witness to a belief that popular education within the parish could open to the laity riches of the liturgy which had been denied them for hundreds of years. It is fatal to imagine that in our own time every Christian knows quite well what the liturgy is and needs only a little encouragement to practice it. The brutal fact is that fifty years after Virgil Michel's death, many parishioners still do not have the faintest notion what the liturgy teaches about God or the human person or the nature of society or the person of Jesus Christ. Since Vatican II an entire generation has grown up deprived of the history and the traditions of Christian symbolism in music and art. It is time to take a second look at the catechetical materials prepared by the liturgical movement in the 1920s and ask how they might be adapted to our own era.

NEW INSIGHTS IN THE NORTH

And yet, if the liturgy would be "the people's work" once again more was required than education. There must be both changes in the celebration of the Mass itself and new opportunities for lay leadership. Virgil Michel gained radical insights into these two areas during the three years he spent away from St. John's Abbey, 1930–1933, in the Indian missions of northern Minnesota. As with the months spent in Europe, this period marks a second time of creative advance. It was during his retirement to the Chippewa Indian reservations that his grasp of the lay apostolate matured, and he came to the conclusion that lay persons must act as leaders in carrying the social implications of liturgy out into the world.

In September 1930 Michel began his life among the Indians with headquarters along Cass Lake. He later moved to the White Earth Mission in 1932 and fanned out from these two centers to work the small mission stations at Federal Dam, Remer, Longville, and Tobique, often braving the blast of the

Minnesota winter by sled in order to arrive at his appointed destination. In the north woods the monk lost some of his prickles and became one of a new American breed of priests—going into saloons to seek out potential parishioners, sleeping and cooking in the open, arriving for worship at one of the stations, covered with dust or snow. He lived with the Indians, hunted deer and bear with them, and adapted himself to their conditions and their standards.

He thus experienced a simpler life, closer to the pain of poverty, than he had lived at St. John's Abbey. He found in this something of a liberation which allowed him to work out actual patterns of co-discipleship among native American laity who were given new responsibilities for instructing the community in the spirit of the liturgy. At the same time there were instances of a return to his old severity in his demand that the Indians adhere to Western Christian standards in some aspects of their lives.

That a monk should need separation from his monastery to grow is one of the common themes of monastic history. We need only think of David Knowles and Thomas Merton in this century or of Jean Mabillon in the seventeenth century or of Aelred of Rievaulx in the twelfth century to be reminded of the importance of liminal experiences if a monk is to become for a moment "the conscience of the Church."[14] For all the support he derived from his abbey, Michel found St. John's by 1930 to be for him stifling in the required busy round of activities thrust upon the monks, stifling in his clashes with Abbot Alcuin, stifling in the hordes of college and prep students, seminarians, and monks all surging together through the confining halls of the one vast monastic quadrangle, stifling in the prayer-life of the monks crowded into one small choir chapel for the recitation of the Divine Office. But in the Indian Missions he found an inner peace that was lacking in his life to this point and a place on the margins of society to rethink the reformation on which he was engaged.

A MORE RADICAL PHASE

When he returned to St. John's in the fall of 1933, Michel now dared to suggest certain reforms that should take place in the practice of worship. There were five parts of his new program: introduction of the vernacular, evening Mass, new postures for the laity at Mass, lay recitation of the Divine Office, and the architectural transformation of Catholic churches:

1. Liturgy in the Vernacular

From 1933 Michel began quietly to advocate a liturgy in the language of the people as a matter of great importance if the active participation of the laity would be carried to a new stage. In 1938 in "The Liturgy in the Vernacular" he made the first public call in the United States for the introduction of English into parts of the Mass: "We should be happy to see the Church go as far as she deems fit in introducing the vernacular into her liturgy. . . . We ardently hope and humbly pray for a more liberal adoption of the vernacular in public worship."[15]

2. Evening Mass

In 1935 the editor of *Orate Fratres* was suggesting what to many was an outlandish, even suspect idea—the celebration of the Eucharist in the evening, following the model of Jesus, so that industrial workers in particular could attend Mass at times convenient to their schedules. By 1937 Michel was pleading for such an arrangement: "The very legitimate question therefore continues to impose itself: Why not an evening Mass. . . . This may be an idle dream. But dreams may also be visions of constructive possibility."[16]

3. New Postures at Mass

After his return to St. John's, *Orate Fratres* began to espouse for twentieth-century Catholics many of the positions taken by early Christians at the Eucharist. *Orate Fratres* contained proposals for the clergy to face the people across the altar during the celebration. There was the suggestion that the laity ought to gather closely about the altar, to become "circumstances," during the recitation of the Eucharistic prayer and that they should bring up the bread and wine to the altar in a revived form of the offertory procession as a reaffirmation of their dignity before God.

4. Architectural Changes

A revival of ancient postures at the liturgy made architectural changes in Catholic churches necessary. From 1933 Virgil Michel began to press for an altar clearly visible and closer to the people. He wished to banish baldachinos, rood screens, heavy Communion rails, side altars, and choir chancels. Such changes would deemphasize the divisions of the space for worship into lay and clerical sections. The new-found unity of the Eucharistic space would focus on the oneness and wholeness of the Body of Christ gathered in the church. The altar would then become the unifying feature of the community, not a sign of contradiction.

5. Lay Participation in the Divine Office

Finally, Father Virgil envisioned a day when more and more of the laity would join in the Divine Office, the official morning and evening prayers of the Church which were then understood widely as the province of the ordained alone. His idea was to reproduce for the people a shortened form of the breviary, the book of the Divine Office, and The Liturgical Press in the 1930s began to bring out pamphlet editions of the hours of Compline and Prime. From 1940 until its revised fourth edition in 1972, the Press's *A Short Breviary* adapted the Divine Office to the needs of the lay person. *A Short Breviary* was anything but short; it contained sixteen hundred pages of Scripture and liturgical extracts. Tens of thousands of lay persons from all across America purchased *A Short Breviary* through the years. More than forty thousand copies had been sold by 1980.

THE LAITY AND LEADERSHIP

The problems of the origins of Christian leadership are tremendously complex and research on these issues today has shown that the earliest Churches witnessed a considerable diversity in patterns of authority, government, and "order." There was a natural assumption of positions of responsibility in the early Church by persons without formal ordination who displayed appropriate gifts of teaching, preaching, healing, and exorcism of evil spirits. A variety of non-ordained forms of ministry and positions of leadership held by those not ordained existed for almost two centuries in the Church and appeared in different cities of the Roman Empire at various times; and there was perhaps even a tendency for itinerant charismatic lay leaders to look down upon local ordained overseers, elders, and deacons.

Gradually in the early Church the influence of these prophets and teachers declined, their unordained office disappeared, and the charisms of prophet and teacher were claimed by ordained presbyters and then subsequently by bishops when the episcopate emerged as a separate office in the second century. Eventually office triumphed over charism everywhere in the Catholic Christian communities, and this has remained the case down to our own day.

However, after 1933 Father Virgil began to stress the importance of a new visibility of lay leadership roles in the Church. His last "Timely Tract," published in *Orate Fratres* only after his death, was a vigorous defense of the revival of the lay apostle as an integral part of the liturgical movement. From 1933 to 1938 he carried on from Collegeville a large and vigorous correspondence with lay leaders who sought his advice and support for their activities.

In addition to these letters, he asserted the possibility of the laity taking on significant leadership roles in other articles for *Orate Fratres* such as "Catholic Leadership and the College" (1935) and "The Scope of the Liturgical Movement" (1936). Here he protests the popular idea that the laity are a "spiritual proletariat" with no intelligent role to play and no responsibility to exercise "except that of a passive obedience like the chess pawn waiting to be moved to the right or the left."[17]

From 1936 to 1938 he was at work on the unpublished manuscript "Liturgy and Catholic Life." Here he wrote at length on the laity, particularly in a fifth chapter on "The Lay Apostle," which contains his most radical thinking on the calling of all Christians as a priestly people. This chapter contains a daring exposition of the lay person as sacrament of Christ: "Every member of Christ is a holy *pharos*, a lighthouse of Christ. . . ."[18] He meant by this that every Christian is responsible for the social environment in which the Church operates. The apostolic lay person must not be aloof from the world. The lay Christian is invested with power and responsibility to share in the work of the Church.

WOMEN AS LEADERS

More remarkable is the fact that Virgil Michel insisted to his contemporaries on Catholic lay women's fundamental equality with men in co-discipleship. He reminded Catholics of the order of deaconesses in the early Church who helped in the administration of baptism, instructed the community during times of persecution, and prepared catechumens for the sacraments. He recalled the double monasteries for women and men, sometimes ruled by women, which had existed in the Middle Ages. In every way possible he encouraged women to participate in the Church's worship and to take on positions of lay leadership since they shared, as members of the Savior's body, in the same priesthood as lay men: "Women are born to be in their own way apostles, not only examples, of Christian ideals and life."[19]

He encouraged the apostolic leadership of three women: Ellen Gates Starr, Dorothy Day, and Catherine de Hueck Doherty. Ellen Starr was a co-founder with Jane Addams of Hull House, one of the pioneer settlement houses among industrial workers in America. More than any other lay person, she was the leader of the liturgical movement among Catholics in the Chicago area. Father Virgil recruited her for his movement and relied on her to be his principal agent in Illinois. She campaigned for lay recitation of the Divine Office, spread pamphlets, brochures, and books through the Midwest, and founded small cells where the laity could meet to pray in community.

Dorothy Day was a second distinguished woman who had a friend in Virgil Michel. He wrote letters to the hierarchy supporting her Catholic Worker Movement, when its leftist tendencies were under attack in the 1930s. Whenever he could he visited Dorothy Day's Houses of Hospitality, a way in which lay people brought the message of Jesus to the streets by feeding the poor and housing the homeless. In the Houses of Hospitality he preached on the Mass as the source of social renewal. When Virgil Michel died, Dorothy Day wrote that "to us at the Catholic Worker, Father Virgil was a dear friend and adviser, bringing to us his tremendous strength and knowledge, for he had such faith in the people, faith in their intelligence and spiritual capacities, that he always gave the very best he had generously and open-heartedly."[20]

A FINAL WITNESS

Catherine de Hueck Doherty was a third woman whose leadership was championed by Father Virgil. When she, along with four other lay persons, began Friendship House in the Toronto slums in the 1930s for work among the unemployed poor, including blacks and communists, they were greeted with disdainful frowns from the hierarchy and indifference and ridicule from other laity.

Catherine Doherty was ready to quit when one morning in 1935 Virgil Michel stepped into the bare room of her empty store front on Portland Street. He sat down on an old broken chair and spoke to her from the depths of his own suffering and experiences of poverty. He discussed the apostolic vocation of the laity, and worship as the basis of Catholic action. He concluded that snowy day amid the depressing cityscape of Toronto:

> How fortunate you are. . . . This is what I have been dreaming about. You are discouraged. You need the Mass. You must persevere by all means. You have a vocation. Study the Mass, live the Mass.[21]

In Catherine de Hueck Doherty's opinion, "Father Virgil foresaw the laity as the spearhead of the Church in coming times. . . . Without him there may not have been a Friendship House movement at all."[22]

When she went to Rome years later as an official delegate of Canada to the first Congress of Lay Apostles, the pope's words to her in a private audience were similar to the encouragement she had heard from Virgil Michel's lips on that snowy day in Toronto twenty years before: "Persevere in your vocation at all costs: the Church needs lay apostles."[23]

NOTES

1. Virgil Michel, "Scope of the Liturgical Movement," *Orate Fratres* X (1936) 488.

2. Virgil Michel, *Orate Fratres* I (November, 1926) 2; Virgil Michel, "The Layman in the Church," *Commonweal* XII (1930) 123–25.

3. 1 Corinthians 10:16; 1 Corinthians 12:25.

4. Virgil Michel, *Orate Fratres* III (January, 1929) 90; Virgil Michel, *The Liturgy of the Church* (New York: The Macmillan Company, 1937) 53, 59.

5. Virgil Michel, *ibid.* 60–61.

6. Virgil Michel, "Editor's Corner," *Orate Fratres* I (1926) 29.

7. Virgil Michel, *Orate Fratres* I (September, 1927) 46.

8. Letter of Justine Ward, May 10, 1925, Archives, St. John's Abbey, Collegeville, Minnesota.

9. Virgil Michel, "Apostolate," *Orate Fratres* IV (1930) 322.

10. Copy of letter of Alcuin Deutsch, September 21, 1935, Archives, St. John's Abbey, Collegeville, Minnesota.

11. *Idem.*

12. Romano Guardini quoted in J. M. Shaw, R. W. Franklin, H. Kaasa, *Readings in Christian Humanism* (Minneapolis: Augsburg Publishing House, 1982) 535.

13. Colman Barry, *Worship and Work* (Collegeville: St. John's Abbey, 1956) 268.

14. Richard Endress, "The Monastery as a Liminal Community," *American Benedictine Review* 26 (June, 1975) 151.

15. Virgil Michel, "The Liturgy in the Vernacular," *Orate Fratres* XII (October, 1938) 566-67.

16. Virgil Michel, "Why Not the Evening Mass?," *Orate Fratres* XI (1937) 30.

17. Virgil Michel, "The Scope of the Liturgical Movement," *Orate Fratres* X (1936) 485-90; Virgil Michel, "The Layman in the Church,' *Commonweal* XII (1930) 123-25.

18. Virgil Michel, MS Liturgy and Catholic Life, Archives, St. John's Abbey, Collegeville, Minnesota, 51.

19. Virgil Michel, "The Liturgical Movement and the Catholic Woman," Central Verein of America: *Annual Report* (1929) 58.

20. Dorothy Day in *Orate Fratres* XIII (January, 1939) 139.

21. Paul Marx, MS Interview with Catherine de Hueck Doherty, February 5, 1953, Archives, St. John's Abbey, Collegeville, Minnesota.

22. *Idem.*

23. *Idem.*

5

The People's Work

> You have your Mass, you have your altars. . . . now go out into the highways and hedges and look for Jesus in the ragged and the naked, in the oppressed and the sweated, in those who have lost hope, and in those who are struggling to make good. Look for Jesus in them, and when you have found him, gird yourself with his towel of fellowship, and wash his feet in the person of his brethren.[1]

These words of an English bishop summarize the last three years of Virgil Michel's life. From 1935 to 1938 he was driven to proclaim a three-part message on the integral connection between Eucharistic worship and a right understanding of the world of work: (1) A liturgy in which all participate turns hearts from self-seeking to a sharing of goods. (2) Communal liturgy challenges popular life-styles in industrial society. (3) The Church in its corporate worship becomes a sign of the justice and peace that God wills for the whole of humanity.

WORSHIP AND JUSTICE

More than any other United States Catholic of the twentieth century, Virgil Michel reminded Christians of the intimate bond between liturgical worship and social justice in the industrial work place. This is his teaching, in part:

The liturgy does not offer a detailed scheme of economic reconstruction. But it does give us a proper concept and understanding of what society is like, through its model, the mystical Body of Christ. And it puts the concept of community rather than individualism into action in its worship and wants us to live it out in everyday life. By ever sowing in men's hearts the seeds of the unifying bond that ties them all to God and to each other in an intimate social fellowship, the liturgy will transmit the solid values of communal civilization.[2]

In 1935 the staff of *Orate Fratres* was reorganized and its policy reshaped to emphasize more strongly the social-justice implications of liturgy. Michel's writings on work from a liturgical perspective come from years when the economic life of the United States had become "hard, merciless, and sinister," in his eyes.[3] Because of the economic depression, 5,000 commercial banks had failed. The number of unemployed industrial workers had reached 15,000,000 by March 1933, and unemployment remained at 10,000,000 until the outbreak of World War II.

Faced with these conditions and judging that the campaign for the active participation of the laity in the liturgy had matured sufficiently, Virgil Michel became absorbed in writing and lecturing on the social implications and the human values of the liturgy. Michel labeled as "the social question" what we today call industrialization. Most secular reformers of the 1930s identified "the social question" with a crisis of wages and the money system. By contrast, to Virgil Michel the social question was not just a matter of economics, to be resolved by secular legislation. Social reconstruction, the answer to the "social question," could only be achieved by restoring an organic structure to society. Here is where *liturgy* would make an indispensable contribution. Virgil Michel asked: could society be transformed unless hearts, souls, and persons were changed first? Spurred by an apostolic vision of society and living communally a renewed spiritual life, whose source was the liturgy, Christians could gradually reform social institutions.

THE MYSTICAL BODY OF CHRIST

The early American liturgical movement, with its core idea of "the Mystical Body of Christ," pointed the way to a program of social action based on spiritual rejuvenation. How did this theological doctrine of the Mystical Body of Christ frame all of the social thought of the liturgical movement and relate to the world of modern industry? All work, all human and Christian life in the contemporary world, should be thought of in terms of the Christian's organic union with Jesus Christ, and with other men, women, and children in Christ. In the supernatural community of "the Mystical Christ" is to be found the pattern and inspiration for social living in an industrial era characterized by fragmentation, isolation, and alienation. This thought runs like a constant theme through all Michel's writing on social justice: the fellowship and communal structure of the Mystical Body as experienced in the Eucharistic liturgy is the best model and guide for all economic organization in an age marked by advanced individualism.

In the last two years of his life, Father Virgil began to outline a practical program to effect a Christian social order in the United States, founded on the insights of the liturgy. This plan included, first, three ideas:

(1) Worker participation in management, ownership, and profits;

(2) A credit system operated for the common good;

(3) Restraint or abolition of irresponsible absentee ownership of factories.

Michel then envisioned four concrete goals for Catholics engaged in social reform:

(a) The creation of industry councils for running factories in which each industrial worker would have a say about the conditions of his or her job;

(b) The promotion of freely organized, autonomous, socioeconomic groups in which each person would have meaningful and emotionally satisfying work;

(c) The elimination of the excessive duties and functions of the secular state;

(d) The foundation of decentralized urban-rural communities in "green belts" where all the material and cultural values formerly associated with highly concentrated industrial-urban populations would be fostered and preserved without some of the dehumanizing characteristics of industrial zones.

FAR-REACHING IMPLICATIONS

In these far-reaching models of Catholic social action, Virgil Michel went beyond all of his Benedictine predecessors in implementing in every way at his command the impulse that leads from participation in worship to involvement in the search for peace and justice in the world. In this he anticipated the spirit of the Vatican II Church and such pastoral documents as *Economic Justice for All*, the 1986 pastoral letter of the United States Catholic bishops. Building on the tradition established in this country by Virgil Michel, *Economic Justice for All* defines liturgy as the principal resource in the Church for a conversion of American Catholics to a deeper reflection on the economic problems of our society. The bishops look squarely at the facts of poverty and hunger but they do not lose hope that the American Church can become "a community of moral purpose."[4] To the bishops, Christian liberation in this country demands economic changes, and these changes require that the nation's Catholics become aware of the moral and social dimensions of our freedom.

In a parallel manner, liberation in concrete terms of political and economic change, undergirded by a fresh perception of Jesus as the liberator from hunger and oppression, is the message of Latin American liberation theology. Like Virgil Michel before them, liberation theologians are keenly aware that needed changes in the social order are not merely external adjustments in economics but require the transformation of the human participants themselves. To Gustavo Gutiérrez, as with Virgil Michel, Christian liberation of the oppressed means forming new men and women and a new society. "The Christian life itself is the passover which allows the transition from corporate sin to grace, from the subhuman to the human," writes Gutiérrez.[5]

To the American bishops, to liberation theologians, to all the followers of Jesus who live in an era still characterized by pressing human problems of enormous dimensions, Virgil Michel beckons us forward to see Christianity as a compassionate perspective on humanity and the world with resources of faith and hope to be applied to the quest for human fulfillment. The very momentum of living the liturgy developed irresistibly "an overwhelming conviction" in him that a genuine liturgical life flows into the whole of culture and human relationships, that Christians must seek "a reconstruction of the social order."[6]

Today the drive toward human unity in many areas of Christian endeavor has underscored the biblical insight that God's creative and redemptive work in the world is intended to bring the children of God together in one community of faith. How to achieve this wider community of God's family, however, has proved to be one of the Church's most difficult tasks. Fifty years after the death of Virgil Michel, though the Eucharist has been restored as a community act of the royal priestly people of God, it is possible to argue that this success has at times been achieved through an easy compromise with an individualistic secular social order which has not been altered by Christianity. There is still a competitive society that too often sets individual against individual, painful economic restriction, and popular forms of culture which exclude the transcendent.

Have we today forgotten important lessons of the American liturgical movement of the 1930s: its effort to teach women and men to find in prayer a meaningful activity with social implications in the midst of economic hardship and its drive to reveal the Eucharist as an act that lifts before us a pattern of more dignified human relationships which actually can be realized in the temporal order?

INTENSE YEARS: 1935–1938

Father Virgil's teaching on worship and justice was developed in an atmosphere of intensity in which he lived again on the edge of society, this time on the border between the world of secular social thought and the realm of the still somewhat isolated Catholic Church in the United States. He enjoyed few things more in the years left to him than the opportunity to engage in discussion with non-Catholic thinkers, philosophers from the University of Minnesota such as Richard Hocking who would drive up to Collegeville for all-night "talk-fests," the small discussion groups that were Father Virgil's favorite form of recreation, and educators such as Scott Buchanan of St. John's College, Annapolis, and Mortimer Adler of the University of Chicago. Adler was amazed at "the breadth of his understanding, cultivated by reading Marx as well as St. Thomas," as the modern monk, following his medieval precursors, sought to bring into one synthesis an analysis of the socio-economic order and the methods of the social sciences with a Catholic social philosophy whose values flowed from the liturgy.[7]

The bruising pace of this last period was a refining fire which brought forth a clear focus on the message of Jesus as it bore on the burning issues of the Depression era, in Michel's words, "the injustices suffered by sharecroppers, the gross discriminations against negroes (even at times within the walls of Catholic churches), economic oppressions of all sorts, crying court injustices, violent vigilante antics. . . ."[8] The courage of his witness must be projected against a dark background in which most American Catholics were saying that nothing was wrong with their economic system and in which the Catholic press was for the most part respectful of the *status quo*.

"His was a voice crying out in what was almost a wilderness of silence and conformity and complacency." These are the words of Mortimer Adler, who went on to say, "He dared always to be true to the principles of Christianity, first and foremost, and to regard the authority of merely human sources as secondary. He never allowed himself to betray these principles by an uncalled-for compliance to local prejudices or institutional shibboleths. He would not become party to any cause which was not the cause of all good men."[9]

A flame was stirred up within him to bear witness to the divine power at work recreating a fatally flawed world; to proclaim that the benefits of the new age which began with the resurrection of Jesus from the dead—life, wholeness, freedom, and peace—could be realized now, on this earth, through the working of God in the community of faith, the Body of Christ, the fellowship of the Spirit, where the more excellent way of love found concrete expression in worship. All who experienced such worship should be led to behold Jesus present in his Word and Sacraments, and to recognize Jesus in the lives of those gathered around the altar.

FINAL DAYS

His activities during his final months illustrate the life of a man caught between two worlds. It was in such a life that Father Virgil saw with the eyes of faith things which were hidden from his co-religionists. For example, in April 1938 he made contact with and visited the Antigonish Movement in Nova Scotia. In this Canadian Maritime Province he saw an ideal Catholic social reform movement in operation, aspects of which he wished to import to the United States. The Antigonish Christian cooperative movement fostered folk arts and crafts, weaving, carpentry, folk dancing, and storytelling to counter the destructive influence of the industrial capitalism being imported into Canada from the United States. This movement preserved craft traditions and handiwork within the sacramental context of the parish. The cooperatives emphasized simplicity and authenticity in work and a preservation in labor of the delight of working with one's hands, of working close to the natural rhythms of the earth. Public activities such as planting a parish garden were powerful witnesses in Nova Scotia to a shared Eucharistic vision of life which balanced spiritual advancement with the preservation of natural beauty.

It was such a joining of the secular with the sacred which Virgil Michel wished he could translate into American parishes. He wanted Americans now to take seriously the call for worthy temporal conditions implied in the physical dimension of the sacraments. He urged his fellow Catholics to become concerned about the waste and the greed of the industrial culture surrounding them. There was, then, an intimate connection between Virgil Michel's concern for the liturgical progress of the American people and his interest in advancing economic democracy. He was convinced that in the Holy Eucharist, God, the creator and giver of life, had provided the means by which life is undergirded and strengthened at its very deepest levels so that it might come to its highest fulfillment in social activity.

His last spring and summer of 1938 were devoted to spreading this message at retreats for Catholic clergy and laity, at secular academic symposia at Northwestern and Notre Dame Universities, and in lecture series before large audiences in such cities as Toronto and Indianapolis. It was the opportunity to hear this unusual point of view coming from a Catholic spokesman which attracted crowds to these occasions, for Father Virgil was by no means an eloquent speaker. His voice was marked by a somewhat annoying exactitude of enunciation and a monotone which revealed little trace of emotion or humor.

The crowds, the diverse audiences, the grinding travel, and the sleepless nights began to take their toll. In August 1938 the weary monk wrote Abbot Alcuin from Toronto: "My eyes are quite granular again and sleep is very spasmodic. . . . I feel mentally all used up."[10]

Three months later Father Virgil fell victim to pneumonia and a streptococcus infection. Perhaps if he had had more reservoirs of strength and resistance to disease—which strength had long been overtaxed in his many and demanding works—or if antibiotic drugs had been in existence then, he would have survived. But life quickly ebbed from his body, and on November 26, 1938, the last day of the liturgical year, Virgil Michel died at the age of forty-eight in the infirmary of St. John's Abbey. Of the expressions of sympathy which poured into Collegeville, none caught more precisely his significance than that which came from his non-Catholic friend Mortimer Adler:

> In the crisis of our times, he saw the need to go straight to the point, leaning neither to the right nor to the left. He was almost alone in this country, in his Christian understanding of the position the Church must take toward fascism and communism in the struggle for a good society. . . . He did this at great expense of time and labor, never saving himself if there was an opportunity to reach other minds through one or another vehicle of communication.[11]

FATHER VIRGIL'S ANALYSIS

The voice was stilled but the message lives on today scattered through three books, nine major pamphlets, and fifty articles which were the result of the labor of these final months. Of these, the most significant titles are *The Christian in the World, Christian Social Reconstruction, Critique of Capitalism, Ideals of Reconstruction,* and *Reconstruction Schemes.*

The relationship between worship and factory work was a central theme of these writings, for to Father Virgil it was the industrial system above all that was pressing the need for American Catholics to rediscover community in the celebration of the Eucharist. If there was a sense of urgency in his appeal it was because he believed that industrialization was rapidly advancing the alienation of his fellow citizens from life in community, and it was separating the spiritual from the material aspects of modern life.

He knew that in preindustrial America time spent on the job had been passed at a slower pace, accompanied by a variety of convivial social practices such as singing and drinking. But now the factory created a new notion of work, and it was not necessarily a pleasant one. Factory workers during the Depression still had to stand alone at their machine, often six days a week. They had to keep up with the machine for endless hours. The factory forced upon women and men a new rigorous discipline which removed them from their families, from parish communities, from easy-going preindustrial habits. Workers complained that they were mere numbers manipulated by a faceless bureaucracy and toiling for the profit of an unknown millionaire. Father Virgil often quoted from the memoirs of such a nameless proletarian, C702, who was reminiscent of Charlie Chaplin's pitiful character of "Modern Times," to illustrate that factory "labor is depersonalized or dehumanized to the nth degree":[12]

> When I entered industry I found it a nightmare of time—recording clocks . . . which impressed upon me that my place in the universe was C702. . . . The machine took hold of me with its iron fingers and worked me into the shape required. . . . attention was lavished on the stresses and strains of machinery and metal, but the more delicate mechanism of human nerve and sinews—not to speak of human souls—was ignored.[13]

Michel did not shrink from pointing to the industrial system as the source of an unhappiness among the working class which was leading to a rise in alcoholism, child abuse, divorce, and a consequent weakening of the social fabric of the nation:

> . . . personal relation has been abolished by the mechanization of labor. . . . this has produced a modern Moloch that swallows all who are its victims either through too abject subservience or through refusal to adore. There is no room left for human elements to have human play, no opening for human affections beyond the initial wonder at the giant creation of man's brain.[14]

WHAT THE TIMES REQUIRED

Christians living in an industrial era characterized by the reduction of communal experiences in daily life thus were required to be shown model communities of the ages of faith, old models which could teach modern people how to keep the fast as well as the festival. It was for this reason that Father Virgil set before the eyes of the American people the then forgotten world of the patristic Church: the intense consciousness of human solidarity expressed in the writings of the Fathers; the fellowship, sharing, and corporate celebration the early Church experienced in its liturgical worship; the essential vision of the patristic Church as that of a community propagating itself in opposition to the dominant pagan power. Like Father Virgil, the Fathers were fully aware that "the liturgy is the indispensable basis of Christian social regeneration."[15]

> They were conscious of the fact that it was impossible to give one's thought and activity to growth in Christ . . . when excessive worry as to the next piece of bread occupied one's attention."[16]

For these first Christian teachers, surrounded by the great masses of the Roman cities, people threatened in their freedom as the secular powers sought to force them into chains, the Eucharist portrayed in a visible way the Christian understanding of the true nature of human society. Their Eucharist was an act which built togetherness and in whose celebration there was no discrimination between high and low and Jew and Greek; their Eucharist made the structure of a human community possible; in their lives the "new creation" was taking shape in the form of economic relationships unlike those of the surrounding secular society.

The Fathers' vision of human life was interpreted by Virgil Michel as offering something better and more enduring for the family and the parish than the secular, materialistic verities of the twentieth century could afford. From the patristic perspective, families that lived according to the liturgy understood their lives in the spirit of pilgrims and did not seek security in material goods alone. In the parish, human work of every kind was understood as a duty of solidarity, a means of social service, never at the expense of another member of the community. Talents, gifts, and goods were to be shared to build up the local Body of Christ.

WHAT FATHER VIRGIL WISHED

It was this spirit of Christian solidarity that Father Virgil above all wished to propagate in the factory world:

> Just in so far as we participate in the liturgy after the mind of Christ do we also live and breathe this supernatural social unity of all members in Christ. . . . The early Christians understood this very well and therefore they had no difficulty in transferring this intimate fellowship of love that was wrought among them in holy Communion into every action of their daily lives . . . such was the sublime lesson of Christian solidarity that was brought home to the early Christians increasingly by their active participation in the liturgy.[17]

Here we are confronted with Father Virgil's frequent assertion that solidarity must bear fruit in love—it must nourish material love, give witness to spiritual love, and discern the ties of communal love in the unity of Christ's body. Thus it is with reason that he so often calls the Eucharist the bond of love. By signs and examples worship should move us from self-devotion to sacrifice for the sake of another. One of the most important gifts of the liturgy, to Virgil Michel, is selfless love for others. Growth in this love makes us feel more strongly the unjust suffering of the innocent and needy ones. He himself experienced this transforming power of the Eucharist as he progressed in his own life from the somewhat forbidding young scholastic to one who ultimately gave his life in the service of others.

At the altar Michel found the answer to the prideful aspects of his own personal life as well as to the sinful aspects of his nation's economic order. He discovered that God wills for proportion and equality to reign among us. Each Christian is to provide for brothers and sisters to the final extent of his means. If that does not happen, the spiritual fellowship of worship is religious delusion and a dangerous deception.

In the end Virgil Michel urged Christians who had been given a radical new vision of human life through the liturgical renewal not to withdraw into a movement apart but to take an active place in their local parish Church. He held that new life could come to every congregation, however routinized into hardened forms it may have become. The local Church is a hearth, and all these rekindled hearts together could gradually make a Christian home on earth again.

Above all, it was the parishes and their members who had to make the case for a new Catholicism in America by living the Gospel radically, by developing in parishioners a critical attitude towards the industrial culture surrounding them, and by making others aware of the dehumanizing aspects of this culture. Through study the parishes needed to foster skills so that men and women would survive in the industrial world as effective and active Christians, capable of making a substantial impact on their Church and their society.

Inevitably the liturgical apostolate merged into an educational apostolate. We must turn now to an examination of the instructional dimensions of the new Catholicism. The manner in which Virgil Michel strengthened the social critique of the liturgical movement by incorporating the philosophy of the papal encyclicals and the scholasticism of St. Thomas Aquinas must now be looked at in some detail.

The People's Work 103

NOTES

1. H. Maynard Smith, *Frank Weston, Bishop of Zanzibar* (London: S.P.C.K., 1926) 302.
2. Letter of Virgil Michel, November 27, 1935, Archives, St. John's Abbey, Collegeville, Minnesota.
3. Paul Marx, *Virgil Michel and the Liturgical Movement* (Collegeville: The Liturgical Press, 1957) 177.
4. National Conference of Catholic Bishops, *Economic Justice for All: Pastoral Letter on Catholic Social Teaching and the U. S. Economy* (Washington: United States Catholic Conference, 1986) para. 63–67.
5. Gustavo Gutiérrez in J. M. Shaw, R. W. Franklin, H. Kaasa, *Readings in Christian Humanism* (Minneapolis: Augsburg Publishing House, 1982) 628.
6. Virgil Michel, *Christian Social Reconstruction* (Milwaukee: Bruce Publishing Co., 1937) 1–2.
7. Mortimer J. Adler, in *Orate Fratres* XIII (January, 1939) 128.
8. Virgil Michel, "Social Injustices," *Orate Fratres* XI (1936) 79.
9. Letter of Mortimer Adler, November 27, 1938, Archives, St. John's Abbey, Collegeville, Minnesota.
10. Letter of Virgil Michel, August 15, 1938, Archives, St. John's Abbey, Collegeville, Minnesota.
11. Letter of Mortimer Adler, November 27, 1938.
12. Virgil Michel, "Critique of Capitalism" (1937), in Robert L. Spaeth, ed., *The Social Question: Essays on Capitalism and Christianity* (Collegeville: St. John's University, 1987) 45.
13. Virgil Michel, *ibid.* 42–43.
14. *Idem.*
15. Virgil Michel, "The Liturgy the Basis of Social Regeneration," *Orate Fratres* IX (1935) in Robert L. Spaeth, ed., *The Social Question* 8.
16. Virgil Michel, *The Mystical Body and Social Justice* (Collegeville: St. John's Abbey, 1938) 53–54.
17. Virgil Michel, "The Liturgy the Basis of Social Regeneration," in Spaeth, *The Social Question* 6–7.

Interior of the quadrangle of St. John's Abbey and University in 1923.

6

The Social Question

Economic liberty has always been as important to American life as political liberty. Even though, beginning in the nineteenth century, socialists and others had tried to discredit what they labelled "capitalism," Americans had never turned away from the liberal commercial society that made them more and more prosperous as the decades passed. Immigrants by the million poured into the United States as if to validate the promise of free enterprise.

This optimistic understanding of the American economic system became sharply unconvincing during the Great Depression of the 1930s. Not immigrants but the unemployed now numbered in the millions. Not increasing wealth but deepening poverty seemed the American hallmark. Newspaper photographs of Americans standing in bread lines contrasted harshly with the hopeful image of the Statue of Liberty. Could it be that capitalism had serious flaws—even fatal flaws?

Virgil Michel set out to study capitalism—not only to locate its flaws but to discover its essence. If American life were to be lived more in harmony with the Gospel spirit, it would be necessary to get to the bottom of the economic disruptions of the 1930s. For this kind of task—hard thinking about basic questions—Michel was well equipped.

To penetrate to the core of capitalism, Michel asked first what it is not, and he answered: "Capitalism is by no means merely a system of private property, nor merely a system of mammonism as practiced by a few unethical individuals."[1] In other words the failures of the American economy could not be blamed simply on the fact that individuals rather than the state own productive property in the United States; nor could they be attributed to the immoral manipulation of the economy by a few powerful capitalists. Both these analyses were popular among critics of capitalism. Michel found them inadequate.

What, then, according to Father Virgil, lay at the heart of capitalism? The definition of capitalism he formulated runs as follows: "An economic system that rests on the priority of production over consumption for the purpose of rationalized profit in a free market and free money system."[2]

The making of profit—without which capitalism would not exist—gave the system its dynamism, but profit as purpose also meant that living must come second if profit comes first. And with this insight Michel explained why Americans in the 1930s were "witnessing in our depression the paradox that we express in the phrase 'want or starvation amidst abundance or plenty.' "[3] Capitalism's logic dictates that when "profits have ceased, production also ceases, regardless of the fact that consumption is lagging way behind the normal satisfaction of natural needs."[4]

CAPITALISM REJECTED?

Faced with the fact that profit rather than human welfare dominates capitalism, would Christians be justified in rejecting capitalism altogether and turning to socialism as a more hopeful economic system? What, in particular, Michel asked, should Christians think about the economic side of socialism, which is "based on the collective governmental ownership and management of the essential means of production and distribution of goods"?[5] His answer was that such an economic system would "take away many individual rights of man, which are really indispensable for his living and acting as a true human person."[6] An extreme form of socialism, Michel pointed out, is communism, which seeks to abolish all private ownership. This could hardly be an acceptable alternative for Christians.

The collectivist model of economic life was more than an abstract possibility in Virgil Michel's time, and the chief exemplar of such an approach was the Soviet Union under the control of the Communist Party. Observing the Soviet system from the capitalist America of the Great Depression, Michel found no hope there. Russian Communism, he wrote, "is as much a triumph of brutal force as Capitalism has been at its worst."[7]

Although Michel thus rejected collectivist alternatives to capitalism, he understood them as "full-blown reactions against individualism,"[8] and about individualism, which he sometimes more bluntly labelled "egoism," he had little good to say. The central motivating force of the capitalist economy—the search for profits—led in this direction: "The spirit of individual profit-seeking is one that frankly fosters egoism, especially when it is sponsored in the name of a free-for-all struggle among men who should be cooperating as brothers. . . ."[9] Moreover, individualism or egoism by its nature militates against "family solidarity . . . the social solidarity of the community . . . [and] public life."[10] What possible room would there be for the brotherhood of man under the fatherhood of God if capitalism continues on this course?

Out of capitalism comes yet another corruption of the human spirit. The pursuit of profit is readily transformed from the primary purpose of economic life to the highest goal of life itself. People move from the desire for material goods to a belief in material goods, becoming materialists in spirit as well as in fact.

Although capitalism brings virtually everyone into its web of materialism, the material benefits of capitalism are not distributed equally. Some persons are much better than others at profit-making; Michel observed that capitalist society tends to "the increasing concentration of economic wealth and power in the hands of the few, and the increasing reduction of the majority to a state of economic helplessness and dependence."[11] This splitting of society into haves and have-nots will naturally have frightening political possibilities if the few rich come to dominate the many poor politically as well as materially.

One can easily paint a bleak picture of the world Virgil Michel saw in the 1930s: capitalism at home, with its attendant evils of individualism, materialism, deterioration of social units, society divided along economic class lines; communism in Russia, with the still greater evils of atheism, denial of human rights, domination of all by a totalitarian state. Was there any source of hope for someone who saw these evils and analyzed them so thoroughly? Indeed there was.

CATHOLIC SOCIAL THOUGHT

Virgil Michel saw hope in a revival of the Catholic tradition of social thought, built on the Gospels and elaborated in the Middle Ages by St. Thomas Aquinas and in modern times in the social encyclicals of Popes Leo XIII and Pius XI.

The encyclical to which Father Virgil returned again and again for guidance and inspiration was *Quadragesimo anno*, issued in 1931 by Pius XI. The title of Father Virgil's 1937 book on this encyclical—*Christian Social Reconstruction*—imitated the English title of the encyclical itself—*On Reconstructing the Social Order*.

In much of Virgil Michel's writing on social justice in the 1930s, he follows the concepts and arguments of *Quadragesimo anno* very closely. This chapter has reviewed his criticisms of capitalism, collectivism, individualism, and materialism; Pius XI made similar criticisms. But both Pius and Michel went beyond criticism to suggest solutions to the desperate conditions of so many people in the 1930s.

In the encyclical Pius promised to "lay bare the root of the present social disorder and at the same time indicate the one way of salutary reconstruction, namely, a Christian reform of morals."[12] Michel enthusiastically agreed when he wrote: "This is indeed the 'one way' in which society can get out of the general chaos in which it now finds itself; it is the one way of producing a more stable order out of the growing disorder, which has been so greatly due to the general abandonment of the moral principles of Christianity."[13]

Michel summarized what modern evils have made of society: "Today not even the blind could deny the un-christian character of our civilization and its growing decay."[14] And although both Pius and Michel recognized that reforms of particular social evils might be possible and forthcoming, they nonetheless believed that without a return to the spirit of the Gospels, "no reforms of social institutions can be of much avail."[15]

SOCIAL RECONSTRUCTION

This call for a revival of the Christian spirit was not directed toward conversion of non-Christians to Christianity, but rather to Christians themselves. As Michel said of Pius's encyclical, it "puts the burden or task of Christian reconstruction squarely on our own shoulders, who are the inheritors of the traditional principles of Christianity."[16]

Invoking "the spirit of the Gospels" does not automatically give concrete directions for a program of social reconstruction. One must understand the moral teachings of Christ and apply them to economic life. "Disorder occurs," Michel wrote, "when the economic life of man is divorced from the control of moral principles."[17] And what are these principles? They are primarily the mandates of justice and charity. Examined in detail, Christian justice and charity would lead to other principles as well, such as "the social duty and responsibility of all ownership, the corporative principles of cooperation in place of strife," etc.[18]

The Christian spirit is a living thing, not merely a list of principles. To absorb this life, a Christian must turn to its source, which, as Michel constantly stressed, is "the solemn and public worship of the Church," the liturgy.

It was important to Virgil Michel to solidify the claim which he and Pius XI made, namely, that true and lasting social reconstruction must be grounded in the Gospels. Naturally he went for further guidance to the first great social encyclical, *Rerum novarum*, issued in 1891 by Pope Leo XIII. Pius had consciously issued his own encyclical on the fortieth anniversary of *Rerum novarum*.

PRIVATE OWNERSHIP

In Pope Leo's time, the mass effects of industrialization on society had become both clear and frightening. As industry produced wealth, the awful condition of many factory laborers became an urgent cause for concern. In the minds of many critics, the system of private ownership of productive property became the enemy against which to struggle, and revolutionary socialist theories, including that of Karl Marx, circulated among Christians and non-Christians alike.

Rerum novarum, however, forthrightly defended private ownership and severely proscribed socialism: "The fundamental principle of Socialism which would make all possessions public property is to be utterly rejected."[19]

But defending private ownership did not entail defending the enrichment of the few owners at the expense of the many who did not own productive property. Pope Leo, after repeating that private ownership is "a right natural to man," asked an important question: "How ought man use his possessions?" Leo replied with a quotation from the medieval theologian and philosopher Thomas Aquinas: "As to this point, man ought not regard external goods as his own, but as common so that, in fact, a person should readily share them when he sees others in need."[20] Here was an idea for a middle way between self-aggrandizement and collectivism—property should be privately owned but used for the common welfare.

Virgil Michel found Aquinas's approach to property issues attractive enough to devote significant time to the study and exposition of the great medieval thinker's ideas. In Michel's 1936 essay "Purpose and Duty of Ownership," he begins by announcing, "I shall proceed to develop my topic by means of quotations from St. Thomas Aquinas which I shall comment upon and expand as occasion may demand."[21] In Aquinas's master work, the *Summa Theologica*, Michel found basic ideas that he could apply to problems such as the purpose of material goods, the basis of private property, the connection of material goods with virtue, the limitations on ownership, etc. These were not only medieval speculations but urgent modern problems.

For example, Michel asked the question, "When has a man more than he needs?"[22] Clearly this is a central question in a capitalist economy where some people grow very rich and the prosperity of some others is constantly increasing. Michel found that Aquinas had answered the question by analyzing the human need for material goods. Aquinas said, "External goods are said to be necessary to us in two ways. One is that amount without which a person cannot exist or live. The other is that which is necessary for us to live honestly or decently, according to our state in life."[23]

From this idea Aquinas—and Michel seven centuries later—drew a conclusion about excess wealth: "Since the use of riches is ordained for the subvention of the necessities of the present life . . . it is patent that he who does not use his riches for the subvention of the necessities of this life departs from virtue."[24] Michel had his answer: A person has more than he needs when necessities broadly understood are satisfied; wealth beyond this limit must be used for the benefit of others.

Virgil Michel's efforts to understand the moral foundations of social justice required serious scholarly labors, as exemplified above, particularly in the Catholic tradition, and more particularly in the papal encyclicals and the works of Thomas Aquinas. But Virgil Michel was never satisfied with scholarship alone, nor with the spreading of his ideas through publication. He wished also to inject his ideas into the manifold realities of everyday life.

THE SOCIAL INSTITUTE

In 1935 Virgil Michel began a series of weekend conferences for men from local Catholic parishes in Minnesota. Co-sponsored by the Minnesota Branch of the Catholic Central Verein and St. John's Abbey, and held at St. John's, the series was named the Institute for Social Study. Lectures, discussions, and liturgy made up the work of the conferences. The goal of the Institute was the education of Catholic laymen in the principles of social justice, laymen whose life and work could put these principles to work.

Michel and his colleagues prepared to welcome a group of about twenty "delegates" one weekend per month during each academic semester. The delegates would be chosen by the local units of the Central Verein, which would share the cost of the weekends. Father Virgil and certain St. John's University professors, along with other invited instructors, would present lectures and lead discussions.

Hardly had the Institute begun in the winter of 1935 when trouble appeared on the horizon. Bishop Joseph Busch of the St. Cloud Diocese, who understood the fledging Institute to be an attempt at "Catholic Action," officially defined as the apostolate of the laity under the direction of the hierarchy, insisted in a letter to Abbot Alcuin Deutsch that any such venture must "conform to the norm set by the Holy See." This norm implied that the local bishop must have control over all Catholic Action in his diocese.

About the Institute, Bishop Busch wrote to the prior of St. John's Abbey (the abbot was on a trip to the Bahamas) on February 11, 1935, requesting that "before these lectures be given, they be submitted to me at least in the form of sketches for my written approval."

Father Virgil found the bishop's request to be an unwarranted interference in an educational venture. Although he immediately agreed to "submit the sketches of the next lectures to His Excellency," Michel also lodged a protest with his prior—"I protest that our project is one of education in social philosophy." To Busch, Michel wrote a similar letter, denying that the Social Institute was training men in Catholic Action: "Ours is a much more modest claim of educating men in the principles of Catholic social thought." The controversy pivoted on the distinction between "education" and "training for action."

Father Virgil was not satisfied with having explained himself to bishop and prior. On the same day he wrote to the bishop, he also wrote to the Benedictine abbot primate in Rome, alleging that Bishop Busch "seems to be intent on considering [the Institute] Catholic Action so that he can step in."

Nor was the bishop satisfied with the sketches of the Institute lectures Michel sent to him. Busch wrote to Michel on February 15, calling one lecture "misleading," another "muddled up," another "purely secular." And about the Institute itself, Busch ominously concluded, "I fear it will do the delegates more harm than good."

Father Virgil was alarmed by Bishop Busch's interference. On February 17 he wrote to the apostolic delegate to the United States, Archbishop Amleto Cicognani, as follows: "We have good reasons to fear that our bishop is intent upon stopping our Institute."

In March 1935 Michel again sent sketches of the Institute lectures to Busch, and again the bishop disapproved: "The religious or supernatural is not stressed as much as it might be and should." It was a fearful time for the new Institute.

Yet ultimately the air cleared. In 1936 Bishop Busch began his own Catholic Action program in the St. Cloud Diocese and henceforth allowed the Institute to be a part of it. Thus after a rocky start did an educational program acquire a practical side as well.

INSTITUTE THEMES

Several of Michel's colleagues at St. John's University joined him in addressing the Institute conferences. Many of these monks and laymen became well known St. John's professors in their own right, including Fathers Ernest Kilzer, Martin Schirber, Walter Reger, Boniface Axtman, Dominic Keller, Godfrey Diekmann, and lay professor Arthur Farley. Many of the lectures were collected in a series of four small books entitled *Social Concepts and Problems, Economics and Finance, Political Theories and Forms,* and *The Mystical Body and Social Justice.* These were bound together in a volume entitled *The Social Problem.*

The themes favored by Michel and his collaborators in the Institute for Social Study ranged from the highly theoretical to the very practical. Michel himself spoke on individualism, human rights, the purpose of ownership, capitalism, the purpose of money, civil power, and the Mystical Body. Capitalism was also a theme of Reger, Kilzer, and Farley. Keller lectured on totalitarianism, Kilzer on democracy, Diekmann and Axtman on the Mystical Body. For the conference delegates, these lectures must have been quite demanding, for they deal thoroughly with complicated information and difficult concepts.

Some of the Institute lectures got down to day-to-day practical matters. Michel spoke on birth control and admitted that "the present economic depression furnishes the strongest reason for artificial birth control," but he asserted his own judgment against that popular one: "It is surely common sense to advocate an economic improvement of the situation of the poor first of all." He went on to attack the use of contraceptives, calling the practice "physically harmful in the long run" as well as a cause of "biological sterility in the woman," and a method of reducing marriage "to the purely biological level."[25]

One weekend conference found Mr. James Dincolo review-
ing the money and banking system in the United States in a
lecture entitled "Credit." The banking system, he said, was
guilty of "notorious and nonsensical policies and practices."
Dincolo echoed one of Virgil Michel's criticisms of capitalism
when he accused lenders of capital of being "predominantly
concerned with the extension of credit for the creation of
producers' goods to the utter neglect of consumers' needs." He
advocated a scheme called "social credit," which entailed put-
ting the credit system into the hands of the federal government: "We must first discharge the present traitorous
manipulators who are recklessly endangering the lives of the
public. Let us replace them with the dignified, omnipotent and
trustworthy Uncle Sam, impartial and unselfish, who will place
a governor on the creation of credit. . . ."[26]

OPPOSITION

When themes such as the faults of capitalism or the advan-
tages of cooperatives were broached at the Institute, some opposition was no doubt inevitable. Thus in October 1936 an
Albany businessman, Henry Blenker, complained to Father Virgil about "too much Co-operative agitation." And writing to
an officer of the Central Verein a month later, Mr. Blenker
was more blunt: "It is just too bad that the Red Propaganda
continues at St. John's Institute. . . . If they want Consumers'
Co-operatives, they should move to Russia; there it is in full
force."

As Michel thought of the Institute as an educational venture, he offered his detractor Blenker the chance to find a
speaker for the Institute "who will present the case against the
cooperatives," but no productive result seems to have been
achieved.

No doubt those delegates who sympathized with Mr.
Blenker's views had not been pleased when, in the winter of
1936, Peter Maurin, the founder of the Catholic Worker move-

ment, had unexpectedly dropped in on an Institute session. Maurin was unwelcome on several Catholic campuses on account of his anarchist opinions. Father Virgil, however, was quite calm: "Peter is *'ein Original'* of the first order," he wrote to the abbot. "But he has a wealth of projects and ideas."

When Father Virgil spoke to the Institute on internationalism, the League of Nations, established after World War I, had proved to be ineffectual. Michel alluded to proposals to give the League the power of sanctions over member nations. But, he said, "There is no earthly source for such authority," i.e., "a central earthly power higher than the sovereignty of individual States."[27] He observed that sovereign nations already operated many international arrangements in the absence of a world-wide authority and he concluded, "The problem in our day, then, is one of not upsetting the balance of these world-wide interrelations, but rather one of working for an even smoother functioning of the same and for consequent greater harmony."[28] Evidently the threatening rise of the Third Reich was not yet visible enough to disturb Michel's optimism in the international arena.

When Michel spoke to the Institute delegates on a community closer to home, the parish, he once again criticized the spirit of individualism for interfering with the valuable community life of a parish. "Only too often the whole supernatural life of individual parishioners is that of a minimum essential contact with the altar, while otherwise they are and remain total strangers to their fellow parishioners. . . ." In contrast he recommended "whole-hearted participation in the official worship of the parish."[29]

Parishes, Michel told an Institute audience, had a special duty toward the poor. As an "intimate element of their very worship of God," Christians are to take care of the needs of the poor "according to their needs."[30] Clearly Michel did not intend his ideas on social justice to remain on the abstract level of academic debate.

SOCIAL JUSTICE TODAY

The special spirit that Virgil Michel breathed into the social thinking of the Catholic Church was revived again in the 1960s, when Pope John XXIII issued the encyclical *Mater et magistra*, published on the seventieth anniversary of *Rerum novarum* and the thirtieth of *Quadragesimo anno*. Pope John repeated and gave new strength to ideas close to Michel's heart, such as the social responsibility inherent in the right to private ownership of property. In a manner that would surely have received Michel's enthusiastic welcome, *Mater et magistra* offered suggestions for practical applications of the principles of social justice, in areas such as agriculture, taxation, social security, price protection, and international economic aid.

In 1965 Vatican Council II issued its pastoral constitution on the Church in the modern world, *Gaudium et spes*. Chapter III of Part II of this document, "Economic and Social Life," develops themes central to Virgil Michel's concerns. For example, the Council expressed its view of the social responsibility of private property: "By its very nature private property has a social quality which is based on the law of the common destination of earthly goods. If this social quality is overlooked, property often becomes an occasion of a passionate desire for wealth. . . ."[31]

Even though the Council spoke to a world long recovered from the Great Depression, the moral problems of modern economic life addressed so vigorously by Virgil Michel continued to need guidance by the same principles he believed in. When the ninetieth anniversary of *Rerum novarum* was celebrated in 1981, Pope John Paul II issued yet another social encyclical, *Laborem exercens*. Pope John Paul sounded again a favorite theme of Michel's, namely, that "the position of rigid capitalism must undergo continual revision in order to be reformed from the point of view of human rights. . . ."[32]

When Virgil Michel is seen in the light of the century-old tradition of Catholic thought on social and economic justice, his ideas may appear commonplace. Indeed, Michel never claimed to depart radically from any part of Christian tradition. Two years after Father Virgil's death, one of his students, Emerson Hynes, who later became a prominent St. John's professor, wrote that in Michel's published writing "there are no outstanding original theories, no careful studies or experiments, and no inclusive syntheses."[33] What then makes Virgil Michel of special significance in the area of social and economic justice?

Any answer to that question would have to refer to the power of Father Virgil's mind and personality and the persuasiveness of his ideas, whether those ideas were original or derivative. Comprehensively and rapidly, Michel took in the ideas and the issues of his age, saw their implications, related them one to another, determined within himself how to cope with them. Zealously he undertook to spread his own ideas and those of the Catholic tradition, through teaching, speaking, writing, publishing. His writing style, not brilliant but powerful, clear, and coherent, was a part of his ability to lead people.

Emerson Hynes characterized Michel: "He was the kind of man whom historians pick out to represent the nonconformists of an era—men who are very much awake to their age and very critical of its defects."[34] Fifty years after Virgil Michel, we can see that the issues he discerned and the remedies he promoted are issues and remedies for our own time. Though very much a man of his era, his social philosophy has transcended it.

NOTES

1. Virgil Michel, *Nature of Capitalism* (Series Four of *The Social Question*), (St. Paul: Wanderer Printing Co., 1937) 16.

2. Virgil Michel, *Nature of Capitalism, ibid.* 16.

3. Virgil Michel, "The Nature of Capitalism," in Robert L. Spaeth, ed., *The Social Question: Essays on Capitalism and Christianity* (Collegeville: St. John's University) 20.

4. Virgil Michel, "The Nature of Capitalism," *ibid.* 20.

5. Virgil Michel, *Reconstruction Schemes* (Series Seven of *The Social Question*), (St. Paul: Wanderer Printing Co., 1939) 6.

6. Virgil Michel, *Reconstruction Schemes, ibid.* 8.

7. Virgil Michel, *Reconstruction Schemes, ibid.* 12.

8. Virgil Michel, *Reconstruction Schemes, ibid.* 5.

9. Virgil Michel, "Critique of Capitalism," in Robert L. Spaeth, ed., *The Social Question, ibid.* 32.

10. Virgil Michel, "Critique of Capitalism," *ibid.* 33.

11. Virgil Michel, "The Nature of Capitalism," *ibid.* 21.

12. Quoted in Virgil Michel, *Christian Social Reconstruction: Some Fundamentals of Quadragesimo Anno* (Milwaukee: The Bruce Publishing Co., 1937) 108.

13. Virgil Michel, *Christian Social Reconstruction, ibid.* 108-109.

14. Virgil Michel, *Christian Social Reconstruction, ibid.* 110.

15. Virgil Michel, *Christian Social Reconstruction, ibid.* 111.

16. Virgil Michel, *Christian Social Reconstruction, ibid.* 112.

17. Virgil Michel, *Christian Social Reconstruction, ibid.* 113.

18. Virgil Michel, *Christian Social Reconstruction, ibid.* 116.

19. Pope Leo XIII, "On The Condition of Workers," in David M. Byers, ed., *Justice in the Marketplace: Collected Statements of the Vatican and the United States Bishops on Economic Policy, 1891-1984* (Washington: United States Catholic Conference, 1985) para. 23.

20. "On the Condition of Workers," para. 36.

21. Virgil Michel, "Purpose and Duty of Ownership," in *Social Concepts and Problems* (Collegeville: The Order of St. Benedict, Inc., 1936) 73.

22. Virgil Michel, "Purpose and Duty of Ownership," *ibid.* 76.

23. Virgil Michel, "Purpose and Duty of Ownership," *ibid.* 77.

24. Virgil Michel, "Purpose and Duty of Ownership," *ibid.* 77.

25. Virgil Michel, "Birth Control," in *Social Concepts and Problems, ibid.* 115-17.

26. James Dincolo, "Credit," in *Economics and Finance* (Collegeville: The Order of St. Benedict, Inc., 1936) 86, 89.

27. Virgil Michel, "Internationalism," in *Political Theories and Forms* (Collegeville: The Order of St. Benedict, Inc., 1937) 86.

28. Virgil Michel, "Internationalism," *ibid.* 85.

29. Virgil Michel, "The Parish, Cell of Christian Life," in *The Mystical Body and Social Justice* (Collegeville: The Order of St. Benedict, Inc., 1938) 21.

30. *Idem.*

31. "Pastoral Council on the Church in the Modern World," in David M. Byers, ed., *Justice in the Marketplace, ibid.* para. 71.

32. Pope John Paul II, "On Human Work," in David M. Byers, ed., *Justice in the Marketplace, ibid.* sec. 14.

33. Emerson Hynes, "The Social Thought of Virgil Michel, O.S.B.," *The American Catholic Sociological Review* (December, 1940) 172.

34. Emerson Hynes, "The Social Thought of Virgil Michel, O.S.B.," *ibid.*

7

Religious Education

$\mathbf{F}$ull and active participation of the faithful in the worship of the Church was an unshakable goal of the liturgical movement. In order to achieve this goal, or even to approach it, was it not necessary that worshipers must understand the liturgy? Certainly Virgil Michel believed this strongly, from early in his career when an American liturgical movement was only a germ of an idea.

In 1929, a Milwaukee priest asked a difficult question of Father Virgil. "Reverend and Dear Father," the priest wrote, "How can the Mass be taught to children of the fifth and sixth grades?" Virgil replied with references to forthcoming articles in *Orate Fratres* but candidly added, "A full answer to your question would mean the writing rather of a book than of a single essay." Indeed, it might mean the writing of several books, both for young people and for their teachers. Virgil Michel was not the sort of man to wait for someone else to perform such a difficult and important task.

But understanding the liturgy, for children and adults alike, meant understanding the Church—its history, theology, spirituality; in short, its spirit. Acquiring such broad understanding was clearly a lifelong process for any Christian, beginning in childhood, never ending. Thus if the liturgical movement

121

THE
CHRIST=LIFE SERIES
IN RELIGION

A new graded series of eight books
in religious education for the children
of Catholic elementary schools

Brochure announcing the Christ-Life Series in Religion in 1934.

was to take root and flourish, a system of religious education must be in place as an indispensable support. Early in his career Michel wrote, "For a full religious life it is not enough to give oneself at stated times to prayer or the attendance at Mass; some time and energy ought to be given also to pondering on the truths of religion, on the rational account that can be given of the faith one professes. . . ."[1]

ROUTINE RELIGIOUS INSTRUCTION

Father Virgil was far from satisfied with the religious instruction common in the Catholic schools of his day. In the United States, Catholic parochial schools had been multiplying ever since the American bishops, assembled for the Third Plenary Council of Baltimore in 1884, had expressed their desire that "every Catholic child in the land" have "the benefit of a Catholic school."[2] Those bishops had also issued a command full of hope and optimism, that every Catholic parish in the nation open a parochial school within two years. The same Council promulgated an official catechism for use in Catholic schools; by the time of Virgil Michel, this question-and-answer book, known as the Baltimore Catechism, had become widely used in Catholic religious education.

Despite the large numbers of Catholic children enjoying the benefits of Catholic schools, Michel was skeptical about the quality of the education within them that relied heavily on the catechism and on textbooks based on the catechism. As early as 1922, he wrote, "Children are often drilled for years in doctrines, laws, regulations, observances, practices, and arguments for their faith only to disclose later on that they are not able to give an adequate answer to the many simple questions regarding religion put to them in practical life."[3]

Nonetheless Michel admitted that some memorization of catechism questions and answers was useful, especially in elementary school, but he opposed "the exclusive use of this method with more developed minds"[4]—such as high-school students.

Even when catechetical instruction was supplemented with liturgical practices, Michel worried that these also could become routine and mechanical. In his words, "Young souls may be marched regularly to the reception of sacraments, to frequent devotions, and still not get beyond the acquisition of external habit. . . ."[5] Something better was needed.

Cathechism answers depended for their validity on the authority of the Church, but such dependence seemed to Michel to contain its own danger: "If religious teaching knows no other motive than that of authority, if it hides its dearth of motive behind the authority of the Church whose coercive power alone is made to lend force to arguments, it may arouse only an instinctive counter-impulse in the human heart."[6] Catholics needed more than routine answers backed by the official Church.

In place of dependence on authority as motivation and on rote and routine as method, Michel recommended "that which enters more deeply into the heart and will of man." Religious education must get at true religion, which is "something mysteriously interior."[7]

Michel saw "the great aim of the instructor in religion" to be "to make religion an intimate possession of those whom he instructs." He suggested that means to accomplish this aim could be found "in the very nature of our religion."[8] These means would include the study of the history of religion, the liturgy, and mental prayer. These three, he wrote, "are as so many avenues through which the soul comes the more firmly to possess its treasure of religious truths. . . ."[9]

RELIGION IN THE PREP SCHOOL

What would be the practical shape of a curriculum based on these goals? Father Virgil, always a practical man, designed a four-year course in religion for his alma mater, the St. John's Preparatory School, where he taught in the early 1920s. He believed high-school students needed a presentation "adapted to the nature of the growing mind." But, he added, "Growing curiosity, however, will not be satisfied until the deeper and instinctively human questions of natural reason receive their answer."[10]

Michel divided each year of the high-school course into four parts: memorization, doctrine, history, and practice or reading. Memorization did not include catechism questions-and-answers, but rather selected devotional prayers and passages from the New Testament. The sections on doctrine were based on the "Catechism of the Council of Trent" as well as textbooks and articles from current periodicals. In history, Michel prescribed moving from the life of Christ in the first year to the history of the Church in the United States in the fourth year. For first-year students, "mental prayer" was featured in the "practice" portion of the course, and in the remaining years, readings "on religious topics and questions" were included.

By the time his students were graduated from high school, Father Virgil expected them to to be able "to give to others an intelligent account of their religion and especially to meet adequately the various arguments that are ever being launched against their faith."[11] Clearly the sequence of courses he designed aimed at teaching young Catholics to become mature, well-informed adult Catholics. Surely the students who studied these four years of religious instruction were likely to become the sort of lay people Michel looked forward to in the Catholic Church.

COLLABORATION WITH THE DOMINICAN SISTERS

In the late 1920s Michel began a fruitful collaboration with the Dominican sisters of Grand Rapids, Michigan, in the writing and publishing of religion textbooks and teachers' guides for grade-school children and others. In the summer of 1929, the Dominican convent sent sixteen sisters, both grade-school and high-school teachers, to St. John's for the summer session to work with Father Virgil.

First Father Virgil and his partners wrote guides to the liturgical year meant to supplement the teaching of the catechism. But soon they commenced work on an ambitious series of textbooks, one for each grade from first to eighth, with plans to continue the series all the way into the college years. The grade-school series was entitled *The Christ-Life Series in Religion* and published in eight volumes. Later *The Christian Religion Series for High School* appeared, as well as *The Christian Religion Series for College*, each in two volumes.

Sr. Jane Marie Murray, O.P., was one of Michel's chief collaborators in this work. Soon after Father Virgil's death, Sister Jane Marie paid tribute to his leadership of this project, which she called "his truly monumental work of the liturgical apostolate among children." She recalled in particular that Michel "took special pleasure and pride in the writing of sections of the children's texts; he delighted in the necessary simplicity of diction and was not satisfied until he had achieved it."[12]

The first-grade text, entitled *God Our Father,* exemplifies Michel's desire to put profound Christian truths into the simplest of language. Page 1 of this small book reads, "God is our Father. He lives in heaven. We are children of God. God loves us and watches over us. How good God is!"[13] This little book moves through the main characteristics of God, God's creation, Adam and Eve, and the story of Jesus' life.

Through the grades, the *Christ-Life Series* texts advance rapidly in their complexity and difficulty. By Grade 6, children reading these books encountered over 150 pages on "The Beginning of the Nation of Israel," which reviewed the history of the Israelites from Abraham to the Babylonian Captivity. The second half of the sixth-grade text summarizes Christ's founding of the Church and ends with short biographical sketches of prominent saints.

Publication of the *Christ-Life Series* was delayed by Father Virgil's absence from St. John's Abbey during the early 1930s, when his failing health demanded a reduced work schedule, though he continued to work on this project even then. In his absence his confrere Fr. Basil Stegmann, O.S.B., and Fr. William Busch of St. Paul Seminary carried on the collaboration with the Dominican sisters. Michel returned from northern Minnesota in 1933, and by 1934 all eight volumes of the *Christ-Life Series* were in print.

The *Christ-Life Series* received some helpful praise from bishops and others involved in catechetical education. In 1935 Bishop John J. Cantwell of the Los Angeles and San Diego diocese wrote to Michel: "These books will not only put religious instruction into the mind of the child but place it in the heart and bend the child's daily actions to union with worship."

Evidently not·everyone approved of the textbooks. In August 1935 Michel wrote to his own Bishop Busch of the St. Cloud diocese: "Could we . . . ask Your Excellency, if you see fit, to give us a letter of encouragement or commendation in regard to the Christ-Life Series, and your blessing upon the work." Possibly because of the timing of this request—a few months after the controversy over the Institute for Social Study—Father Virgil got no encouragement from Bishop Busch.

TRAINING TEACHERS

The work of Father Virgil and the Dominican sisters also resulted in the publication of teachers' manuals to accompany the grade-school textbooks. These two volumes contain essays on the teaching of religion, detailed suggestions on classroom techniques, outlines of the doctrines covered in the texts, lists of suggested readings for both children and teachers, and detailed suggestions for guiding children through the liturgical year.

The teachers' manuals emphasize that the teaching of religion at the elementary-school level should be more than the conveying of religious information to children, that it should stress the formation of children's religious lives. For example, the manual asserts, "While talking about preparing children for life, we have neglected to help them to live fully and perfectly in childhood. We have been more concerned with teaching our children to know their religion than with teaching them to live it."[14] This certainly stood against the catechism habit of the era.

This theme—"making religion not merely something to be learned but, rather, something to be lived"—led naturally to emphasis on the liturgical year. Teachers were urged to make the celebration of each liturgical feast "an actual experience for the children, one in which their life in Christ will be increased."[15]

The teachers' manual also recommends combining the study of religion with other subjects in the grade-school curriculum, including literature, music, nature study, art, and dramatics. Although the manual says, "Literature lends itself particularly well to correlation with religion," teachers are nonetheless warned to be on guard against "using stories which are pietistic and which savor of sentimentality. Such stories create false impressions of the real nature of religion and our worship of God."[16]

Since the first-grade text treated God's creation of the world and mankind, it was necessary to treat the subject of sin, always a difficult matter for presentation to children age six or seven. The blunt, even harsh, approach to sin in both text and teachers' manual reveals that the authors of the *Christ-Life Series* permitted neither themselves nor their readers any compromise in the understanding of the realities of Christian life.

The text itself informs the first-graders that God told Adam and Eve not to eat the fruit of a certain tree but that they ate it anyway simply because they wanted to. The text characterizes their willful act: "Adam and Eve disobeyed God. . . . They did something which God had said they must not do."[17] The act of disobedience, the text says, is called a sin, and for this sin Adam and Eve were severely punished.

Along with telling the story of Adam and Eve's sin of disobedience, the first-grade text makes this generalization: "To love God means to do what He wants us to do."[18] In the teachers' manual this identification of loving God and obeying God is made more explicit. Teachers are urged to convey the idea that "God looks at each of you who are here, and he can tell how much you love him by the way you obey him." Disobedience is the only sin introduced at this stage of instruction, and teachers are told to "help the children to realize the heinousness of sin."[19]

Despite these blunt warnings about punishment for disobedience—-and by extension for all other sins—God's great love for God's people is strongly stressed in both text and manual. The title of the third-grade text is *The Story of God's Love* and consists of stories from both Old and New Testaments; its purpose, the teachers' manual says, is "to acquaint children with the evidence of the infinite love of God for man as it appears in the story of his dealings with his creature man."[20]

HIGH SCHOOL AND COLLEGE

The Michigan Dominican sisters and Father Virgil, as well as several of his own confreres, continued to collaborate after the *Christ-Life Series* was complete. But the forthcoming high-school and college textbooks—each much larger than the grade-school texts—were not published until after Father Virgil's sudden death in November 1938.

In the summer of that year, Father Virgil wrote to propose publication of the advanced texts by the New York publishing firm, Benziger Brothers. He assured Benziger that the books "will be tried out in at least ten different schools in different states." In October 1938 Benziger agreed to publish the series, and in the same month that Father Virgil died the firm agreed with his suggestion to divide the royalties equally between Michel and the Dominican sisters.

The Life of Our Lord and *Christ in His Church* were meant for high-school students, while *Our Life in Christ* and *The Christian in the World* were intended for college courses in religion.

According to Michel's co-author Sister Jane Marie, the last-mentioned book reveals more of Father Virgil's own thought than any of the others. "It is in *The Christian in the World*," she wrote, "that Father Virgil's grasp of the whole Christian synthesis receives its most complete expression, I believe. . . . The natural dignity of the human person is set forth with clarity and reverence, as the basis upon which God builds the supernatural."[21]

The Christian in the World reads like a summary of Virgil Michel's understanding of human society and his version of the Christian response to social problems. For example, the chapter entitled "The Social Nature of Man" reviews the ideas of both Aristotle and Aquinas on this subject, then continues with sections on social cooperation, human rights, equality, justice, organization, and authority. It concludes with a section on the Mystical Body of Christ that ends with statements on the importance of the Church's liturgy. The vast topics of this chapter—one of sixteen in the text—are treated in just ten pages.

Although *The Christian in the World* was written as a textbook for religious instruction, it ranges far beyond the conventional understanding of religion. Michel covers topics such as the duty of wealth, the purpose of the state, nationalism, evolution, materialism, totalitarianism, etc. Students who studied from this text surely were educated very deeply and broadly in their Catholic faith and a great number of related matters. It was part of Virgil Michel's special genius to be able to make connections among all the various topics as well as connections between them and Christian faith.

Father Virgil concludes *The Christian in the World* with a grim assessment of the current condition of human society: "Modern life and its civilization have been built on the self-sufficiency of man without God." From this assessment his advice follows immediately: "There must be a return to God and away from the pagan concept of the sufficiency of man unto himself."[22] Although perhaps not deliberate, Michel's conclusion to his most advanced religion textbook is a reminder of the description of Adam and Eve's sin in the first-grade text of the *Christ-Life Series*. There, after eating the forbidden fruit, Adam and Eve, like the materialists and individualists of the modern world, were said to be "children of God no longer. They could no longer see God."[23] And the creation story, like Father Virgil's advanced text, concludes with a promise that a Savior will come to save humankind—but the descendants of Adam and Eve must, as their first parents failed to do, willingly turn toward God rather than away from Him.

THE LAITY

By the 1940s it would have been possible for a young Catholic to have studied his or her religion in every year of school from first grade through the undergraduate college from textbooks written or co-written by Virgil Michel. What sort of Catholic did Michel wish to be the end-product of this religious education? This question can be answered by looking into the expectations Michel had for the ideal Catholic layperson.

Certainly informed and active participation, in both liturgical worship and social action, played a major role in Michel's expectations for the Catholic laity. As he wrote in *Commonweal* in 1930, "There is nothing farther from the Catholic conception than that the ordinary Catholic be only a blind follower or an unintelligent believer in the Church."[24] These expectations were grounded in Michel's belief in "the general priesthood of the faithful," which brings the laity into partnership with the clergy in liturgical worship.

A layperson as well as a priest is a full member of the Mystical Body of Christ. Both are capable of such great benefits from the liturgy that after full participation in the Mass, in Michel's words, "Thereafter they could not but go out into the day breathing everywhere the inspiration of Christ." This kind of layperson, "by the very example of his general conduct," could inspire others to imitation.[25]

Such a layperson's religious education would also be brought to bear on his or her daily social, political, and economic life. Michel recommended that "he can exercise his apostleship by opportunely answering questions, discussing problems in the light of Catholic truth, or, on occasion, by correcting prevalent false impressions."[26] This expectation is very large; to carry it out thoroughly a Catholic would require the kind of religious education Michel worked so hard to design and put into practice.

CATECHETICS TODAY

Has Virgil Michel's work in religious education had any lasting effect? Certainly the rote question-and-answer method of catechetics disappeared from Catholic schools after Vatican Council II, which called for a reform of catechetical teaching. In the decades after the Council, many Catholic students dispersed into the public-school system, thus placing much more responsibility on parish Confraternity of Christian Doctrine (CCD) classes as well as directly on Catholic parents. Even to get the attention of young Catholics for education in their religion has become much more difficult since Virgil Michel's time.

In 1979 the United States Catholic Conference published a "catechetical directory" entitled *Sharing the Light of Faith*, designed to guide parents and teachers responsible for religious instruction. In this work can be found echoes of the central concerns of Virgil Michel, in particular in the directory's emphases on the liturgy and social justice.

A chapter of the directory entitled "Catechesis for a Worshiping Community" asserts that catechesis "prepares people for full and active participation in liturgy . . . and at the same time flows from liturgy, inasmuch as, reflecting upon the community's experiences of worship, it seeks to relate them to daily life and to growth in faith."[27] Using words much like Father Virgil used, the directory calls the liturgy the "heart of the Church's life" and asserts that it "leads its members to seek justice, charity, and peace."[28]

The chapter of the directory called "Catechesis for Social Ministry" defines social justice: "the concept by which one evaluates the organization and functioning of the political, economic, social, and cultural life of society." Social justice must be brought to bear on numerous contemporary issues, the directory says, including welfare and defense policy, capital punishment, racism, "encroachments on basic rights by the federal and state governments and courts," poverty, unemployment, prices and wages, agricultural policy, housing, etc. "The fundamental concept underlying the social teaching of the Church," the directory points out, is the dignity of the human person.[29]

The Catholic bishops of the United States have shown their concern for social justice not only by urging that it be taught in catechetical programs but also by taking their own stand on some of the most difficult social issues of contemporary times. Their pastoral letters on nuclear weapons and the American economy, published in 1983 and 1986, prominently exemplify the bishops' active involvement in the vast social problems of our time. In this activity we can see carried out what Virgil Michel expected also of educated Catholic lay people. The pastoral letters, as well as many other episcopal teachings, are becoming a standard part of religious education in both Catholic schools and CCD classes.

Despite Virgil Michel's influence and despite the reforms of Vatican Council II, there remain deep problems in Catholic religious education today. The fact that the national enrollment in Catholic elementary and high schools plummeted drastically between 1960 and 1980 has made it virtually impossible for most young Catholics to devote sustained attention to the study of their religion. Catholic students in the public schools receive religious instruction at home and in parish CCD classes, but neither of these approaches is likely to offer the broad and deep religious education found in the textbooks of Virgil Michel.

Moreover, as moral problems facing young people have intensified, the official Church's answers to moral and other questions increasingly come into competition with the values of other people and institutions in society. Young Catholics are exposed to influences and arguments that range over many religious outlooks as well as to nonreligious and even irreligious ideas.

No doubt Virgil Michel would today continue to call for the return of everyone to God, to an abandonment of materialist and self-centered ways of life. But how he would approach the religious education of the Catholic youth who are subject to so many distracting influences, both good and bad, is difficult to imagine. Probably the spirit of Virgil Michel would call upon us to find ways to spend much more time with our children and students on their religious education. The content of this religious instruction might be little different from that found in his now forgotten series of textbooks.

NOTES

1. Virgil Michel, "Religion for Credit," *The Catholic Educational Review* 21 (1921) 469.

2. Hugh J. Nolan, ed., *Pastoral Letters of the American Hierarchy, 1792–1970* (Huntington, Ind.: Our Sunday Visitor, 1971) 175.

3. "A High School Course in Religion," *The Catholic Educational Review* 22 (1922) 414.

4. "A High School Course in Religion," *ibid.* 414, n. 2.

5. "A High School Course in Religion," *ibid.* 408–409.

6. "A High School Course in Religion," *ibid.* 409.

7. "A High School Course in Religion," *ibid.* 410, 414.

8. "A High School Course in Religion," *ibid.* 415.

9. "A High School Course in Religion," *ibid.* 415.

10. "A High School Course in Religion," *ibid.* 473–74.

11. "A High School Course in Religion," *ibid.* 483.

12. Sr. Jane Marie, "Father Virgil and 'The Christ-Life Series in Religion,' " *Orate Fratres* XIII (1939) 107, 109.

13. Virgil Michel, Basil Stegmann, and the Sisters of the Order of St. Dominic, *God Our Father* (New York: The Macmillan Company, 1934) 1.

14. Virgil Michel, Basil Stegmann, and the Sisters of the Order of St. Dominic, *The Christ-Life Series in Religion Teachers' Manual* (New York: The Macmillan Company, 1934) 2.

15. *Teachers' Manual, ibid.* 10.

16. *Teachers' Manual, ibid.* 12.

17. *God Our Father, ibid.* 28.

18. *God Our Father, ibid.* 25.

19. *Teachers' Manual, ibid.* 55–56.

20. *Teachers' Manual, ibid.* 105.

21. Sr. Jane Marie, "Father Virgil," *ibid.* 111.

22. Virgil Michel, *The Christian in the World* (Collegeville: The Liturgical Press, 1939) 235–36.

23. *God Our Father, ibid.* 30.

24. Virgil Michel, "The Layman in the Church," *Commonweal* XII (1930) 124–25.

25. "The Layman in the Church," *ibid.* 124–25.

26. "The Layman in the Church," *ibid.* 125.

27. *Sharing the Light of Faith* (Washington: United States Catholic Conference, 1979) 66.

28. *Sharing the Light of Faith, ibid.* 83.

29. *Sharing the Light of Faith, ibid.* 93, 95, 96.

8

Catholic Higher Education

In every aspect of Virgil Michel, whatever work he is pursuing, there is found his idealistic side as well as his hard-headed practical side. He often expressed the best he thought desirable for people to achieve, and at the same time he set about to put into existence practical arrangements to make at least some of the dreams come true. Occasionally he tried to put idealistic elements directly into his practical plans. In no other field of endeavor can these two sides of Father Virgil be seen so clearly as in his efforts to reform college education.

After returning to St. John's Abbey from the Catholic University of America in 1918, having earned a Ph.D. in English, Michel taught English and philosophy in St. John's University. He also served as dean of the Prep School in 1922–1923 and dean of the University in the following year. In 1925, upon returning from his European studies, he resumed the teaching of philosophy in the University. Despite his many other demanding projects, Father Virgil always taught courses when he was in residence at St. John's.

In that era colleges in America struggled with a dilemma that besets them again today. The problem was one of mis-

Virgil Michel as dean of St. John's University in 1933.

sion: should an American institution of higher learning devote its energies to preparing students in the practical requirements of professions and careers or should it emphasize what, in John Henry Newman's words, was called "liberal education," the education of the intellect? St. John's could not escape this dilemma in the 1920s and 1930s any more than Catholic colleges can escape it in the 1980s.

By 1920 the student body of St. John's, numbering about four hundred, was composed of young men whose families by and large had not known the benefits of higher education and whose striving for a decent life moved them to seek practical benefits of all schooling. College education taught students, as it does today, that they would have to choose between alternatives both quite desirable—practical education and liberal education.

Virgil Michel, drawing upon his own advanced education in the United States and Europe, and upon his experience as a classroom teacher, took this dilemma very seriously. His thoughts anticipated many future American Catholic attempts to think through the true purposes of an undergraduate education and the means for achieving those purposes. In 1926 Michel published an extraordinary article in *The Catholic Educational Review* laying out in some detail the ideals he had come to believe. More than sixty years after its appearance, this essay, "Utopia Rediviva"—its title means "utopia revisited"—can still serve as valuable guidance for educators trying to do the best for their students.

The use of the word "utopia" in the title of this article signified that Father Virgil would boldly attempt to lay out what he saw to be the highest and best goals for higher education regardless of how difficult they might be to accomplish. Yet in dividing education into matter and method—that is, the content of what is taught in college and the means used to teach it—his discussion of ideals included practical possibilities as well.

CULTURAL OR UTILITARIAN EDUCATION?

Michel had observed that American colleges tended to over-emphasize utilitarian education at the expense of cultural education. "Cultural" was Michel's word for the philosophical, intellectual education also called "liberal education." Yet he believed, "There are indications that the pendulum is swinging back to a better appreciation, nay to an earnestly felt need, of the cultural over against the *merely* utilitarian, therefore of the cultural *alongside* the utilitarian, in our education."[1] Encouraging this new trend back to liberal education became one of Father Virgil's goals in his professional life as a college professor and administrator.

Michel understood culture broadly—the natural sciences as well as classical literature, mathematics as well as "history in all its wider human aspects, embracing everything that is included under social studies."[2] But it was philosophy, also understood broadly, that he placed at the heart of a cultural or liberal education:

> Nor can we any longer consider philosophy to be exhausted by logic, ethics, or an introductory course in problems, or a historical survey. The course must go deeper and attempt to get more down to the bottom of problems. Nothing less than the attempt to get to the end of things will satisfy the spirit towards which we are tending.[3]

Michel's wish that education would "get down to the bottom of things" expresses in a mundane way his highest ideals. College students should probe deeply into the most serious and difficult problems of life and the world. Why? Because, Michel wrote: "None of the fundamental problems of our life are to-day 'settled'. . . ." These are problems that "enter into the very foundation of our existence, that reach into the very structure of human society, and into the relations of man to God."[4] Clearly this kind of college education goes far beyond preparation for a profession or career, no matter how important that might be in the life of an educated American.

MATTER AND METHOD

Michel observed that most American colleges aimed too low in deciding what subject matter to include in their curriculum; he also found them to be rigid and mechanical in their teaching methods. He asked rhetorically:

> . . . is it not inherently ridiculous that even in our greatest and best teachers' colleges and in universities a professor's secretary enters the assembly hall surreptitiously and records the absences and presences day for day just as a rancher might count his oxen and sheep when he has successfully corralled them?[5]

Michel urged that college teaching methods be "demilitarized, demechanized." Yet he also criticized the elective system where a student can choose from many courses in a curriculum but after choosing "comes under the care of specialists" and the student "learns to see with the eyes of others, and to think the thoughts of others."[6]

Michel's recommendations for better methods in college teaching began conservatively. He believed that in the first two years of college—the junior college as he called them—students should take survey courses in fields such as rhetoric, languages, literature, history, mathematics, and science. Such courses provide "a good opportunity for drill in thoroughness, and for better mastery of the general fundamentals of a cultural education."[7] They would also make up for the deficiencies of the typical high-school education.

However, in such survey courses, Michel stipulated, students ought not to be spoon-fed, but rather the instructor should give "tangible shape and power to what is in the student mind amorphous and scattered in its energy."[8] This respect for the abilities of students gave them great responsibility for their own learning and placed special responsibilities on college teachers as well.

Michel's recommendations for "senior college" students were more daring. In this advanced part of the college curriculum, "The student would choose the subjects he desires to work at, therefore the professors on whose guidance he shall have some claim." The advanced work would have no prescribed subject matter; students would only be required to prove that they "had successfully entered into the purpose of the college—study of the problems of life."⁹ Students would, by the time of their final year in college, take charge of their own education.

Father Virgil realized that his "scheme must seem utopian to the average mind of today," but he did not agree that it was completely impractical. In the Middle Ages universities in Europe had operated successfully using the methods he was suggesting for contemporary American colleges. In those centuries, Michel admitted, the universities were effective partly because "students fought for the privilege of learning" and had "a very passionate hunger for knowledge."¹⁰ But he also believed that at least some people in the modern world had the same passion for learning, and that belief convinced him that at least a few colleges could put his ideals into practice. Possibly one of these could be St. John's University.

INTELLECTUAL INDEPENDENCE

What special intellectual virtues would a student acquire from the kind of liberal education Virgil Michel advocated? In his 1926 essay, he made a provocative remark about students, namely, that "ultimately real education must be self-propelled, and self-impelled to the greatest extent possible."¹¹ The following year he devoted an entire essay to his hopes for college students; he gave it the appropriate title, "Stimulating Intellectual Independence in Senior College Students."

Once again, in this essay, Michel spoke disparagingly of the mechanical aspects of typical college teaching methods. He was tempted to "see nothing in our education but force, compulsory attendance, rigorous supervision of hours and minutes, promotion by quantitative standards, etc." All these mechanisms were inconsistent with "the spontaneous growth of mind that is true education." But, Michel reported with approval, colleges seemed to be currently reacting against mechanical methods with a "spirit of new adventure in education."[12]

Both the dull mechanisms and the new attempts at freedom convinced Michel to consider once again "what we *are to aim at* in education."[13] Here once again we glimpse the essential Virgil Michel: never satisfied with trends and countertrends or with temporary solutions to current problems, but rather determined to get to the root of unsatisfactory conditions, whether in education or economics or religion, to discover the true principles of reform.

Michel was convinced that a college student ought to aim at intellectual independence. But the concept of independence itself smacked of capriciousness and thus could give rise to misunderstandings. True intellectual independence would mean "not independence of thought from fact, nor independence of factual values from interpretative thought; not independence of a chosen field of study and opinions from all else in the world, from their further implications." These misshapen forms of independence were distortions of the real thing. True independence of mind, according to Michel, must "include knowledge of all the major opinions regarding the problems of the day, and of their historical solutions; and only then, the holding of one's own opinions for reasons understood by oneself, independently of the mere dicta of other persons."[14] In short, to become intellectually independent requires the personal discipline to acquire a great deal of knowledge; the knowledge in turn gives a student the right to his or her own opinions.

In this essay Michel returned to the second consideration of his "Utopia Rediviva," the methods of achieving his lofty aims, in this case the goal of independence of mind. For senior college students, he praised the "study-plan system," which offered students the opportunity to study a subject on their own, using their instructors as consultants. But he did not consider this system to be sufficient. In addition, he recommended "broad courses of synthesis":

> . . . for instance, courses in the historic manifestations of democracy (theory and practice); in contemporary religions, their thought and practice; the place of science in modern civilization; cycles of art in the life of man; social economy in ancient, medieval, and modern times, etc., always with a study of causes and implications, not a mere mention of data alone.[15]

Such courses were to be comprehensive and profound; they were intended to stimulate intellectual independence. Michel wrote: "Unless a mind has been thoroughly convinced of the need and the joy of these lessons of experience, it is not, to my way of thinking, intellectually independent; it is either set like cement, or as wayward as mercury."[16] The path to true intellectual independence was a middle way.

CULTURED TEACHERS

If college students are to aim at independence—and practice it to a degree—some special qualities would be expected in their teachers. In "Utopia Rediviva," Father Virgil said that his ideal college would require not more teachers but "perhaps teachers of wider experience in the things of mind and soul, possessing the optimism of a sound faith in the things of God and man." They should be "broadly cultured teachers of wide sympathy and human understanding."[17] He imagined a college faculty as John Henry Newman did in the nineteenth century, and he quoted a passage from Newman's *Idea of a University* to show what he hoped for:

> This I conceive to be the advantage of a seat of universal learning, considered as a place of education. An assemblage of learned men, zealous for their own sciences, and rivals of each other, are brought, by familiar intercourse and for the sake of intellectual peace, to adjust together the claims and relations of their respective subjects of investigation. They learn to respect, to consult, to aid each other. Thus is created a pure and

clear atmosphere of thought, which the student also breathes. . . .[18]

"A pure and clear atmosphere of thought"—this inspiring phrase of Newman sums up the ideal of the liberal arts college Virgil Michel aspired to. The faculty must be capable of producing such an atmosphere, and by breathing it, the students could become independent thinkers, because, Michel wrote, "true intellectual independence, seems to me to come chiefly from contact with minds possessed of it." The teachers in this ideal college would be "models of the truly cultured, balanced, independent mind."[19]

And what would be the relationship of the faculty to the students? Michel answered: "Association between instructors and students would have more of the nature of informal intercourse between men of kindred ambitions, which is the best type of social intercourse." These teachers might give lectures, but not the kind experts give to passive listeners. Their method would mostly consist of "the good old Socratic way of questions."[20] In other words, the students would enter into a partnership of learning with their instructors. Like Socrates' students, they would be subjected to hard questioning, the kind designed to lead on to deeper and deeper problems in human understanding.

During the late 1920s, when Father Virgil wrote these essays on liberal education, he was extremely busy—perhaps too busy—with other projects also. The Liturgical Press and *Orate Fratres* both were launched in 1926, and the writing collaboration with the Dominican sisters began in 1929. In the same period Michel translated several books from French and German into English, including Beauduin's *Liturgy, the Life of the Church*, and Grabmann's *Thomas Aquinas: His Personality and Thought*. Michel's articles and reviews numbered over twenty per year at this time. Small wonder that this overworked man had to take an enforced rest; he spent the years from 1930 to 1933 in the Indian missions in northern Minnesota.

RENEWED ENERGY

In 1933 Michel returned to St. John's as dean of the College of Arts and Sciences. He had five years to live; in that period he pursued his multifaceted vocation with renewed energy. Among all the rest of his projects, he resumed teaching. By 1936 he had designed a special two-year course for upper-division college students that aimed to put his ideals into practice in his own classroom.

"Sociology 47-48" was a modest label for Michel's course entitled "Catholic Backgrounds and Current Social Theory"; the label is misleading today, for the term "sociology" has changed in meaning. Then it could mean a broad and multi-disciplinary study of society while today it is a technical term for a scientific approach to social groups. In his mimeographed syllabus for the course, Father Virgil stated its ambitious purposes:

> [This course] will endeavor to convey a mastery of the best Christian thought of the day, with particular reference to forward-looking ideas and programs in regard to every phase of social and cultural reconstruction.

This course provided Michel the opportunity to bring to bear in the classroom his broad education in Europe and the United States, along with his concerns for the social reconstruction advocated by Pope Pius XI in the encyclical *Quadragesimo anno*.

Michel's detailed syllabus indicates that "Sociology 47-48" was marked by depth as well as breadth. The topics for the course were listed as follows:

1. The Writings of the Christian Sociologists.
2. The Personalist and Communitarian Movements.
3. The Writings of Christopher Dawson, Maritain, e.a.
4. Corporate Order vs. Totalitarianism.
5. The Catholic Revival of Our Day.
6. The Theological Basis of Sociology.
7. The Liturgical Movement.

8. Social Life and Ideas of the Middle Ages.
9. The New Money Theories.
10. The Agrarian Movement.

Writings of prominent European Catholic philosophers and historians besides Christopher Dawson and Jacques Maritain were read in the course, including Emmanuel Mounier, Nikolai Berdyaev, Francois Mauriac, Hilaire Belloc, G. K. Chesterton, and others.

The course syllabus for "Sociology 47–48" also indicated Michel's efforts to turn his ideas on the proper method of teaching in college into practice. About his course, he wrote, "The work of the curriculum shall be conducted entirely on the basis of mutual cooperation and exchange, after the ideal set down by Cardinal Newman for a true university." Students read, wrote papers, and were expected to participate in discussions in the classroom and outside it. Michel gave very few lectures.

This course syllabus was actually a large collection of reviews of the assigned books, summaries of lectures by various members of the faculty, extensive bibliographies, discussion questions, and copies of student papers. It appears today as a complete history of the course, and it is tangible evidence of the amount of work that Virgil Michel put into his teaching. To spread his practical ideas about teaching, he distributed copies of this syllabus far and wide.

REFORM OF LIBERAL EDUCATION

Not content with reforming his own classes and his own teaching methods, Michel made plans for a radical change in the first two years of the St. John's University curriculum. For inspiration and ideas he turned to the founders of the great-books plan of college education, in particular Mortimer Adler, professor of philosophy at the University of Chicago.

Adler, along with Robert Hutchins, Scott Buchanan, Stringfellow Barr, and others, believed as Father Virgil did that reform of college education meant a return to the best available sources of human wisdom, the most powerful and influential writings of the Western tradition. In 1937 Michel began a correspondence and a friendship with Adler. Each visited the other on his home grounds. Their many letters often recommended recent books and articles, and each could be sure the other would read them.

In February 1938 Michel asked Adler to give the commencement address at St. John's University that spring. Adler graciously replied: "I shall be delighted to accept your kind invitation to give the commencement address at St. John's on the afternoon of Sunday, May 29. It will be a pleasure indeed to return to the lovely surroundings of the abbey."

During the same period as Michel's planning for a reform of the St. John's University curriculum, Barr and Buchanan respectively became president and dean of a small secular college in Annapolis, Maryland, also named St. John's. There, in 1937–1938, they put the great-books idea of education into practice, devoting the entire curriculum to what Michel had called "cultural" education and abolishing many of the features of American colleges that Michel also opposed, including pre-professional training, elective courses, lecture classes, etc. Michel visited St. John's of Annapolis to see the program in operation and to consult with those who were shaping it.

GREAT BOOKS

Adler was prominent in the planning that led to the St. John's College "new program." And on September 13, 1938, he responded to a request from Michel with a nine-page letter recommending in detail how Michel might begin a similar program in Collegeville in the fall semester of 1939. In this letter, Adler laid out a curriculum for a great-books program for the freshmen of St. John's University.

The program, he said, falls into two parts: (1) "The Reading of the Classics: *Seminars and Lectures*"; and (2) "Proficiency in the Liberal Arts: *Reading and Writing Tutorials, Mathematics and Greek Tutorials.*" Michel intended to use Adler's advice to consult with the faculty during the academic year 1938–1939 and to implement the new program in the fall of 1939.

Adler's detailed letter makes suggestions for the content of the various seminars and tutorials, which would take up about two-thirds of a student's time, leaving time for a traditional major field of study. All of the readings for the freshman program were to be chosen from the literature of ancient Greece and Israel. The seminar would discuss Homer, Herodotus, Thucydides, selections from the Old Testament, Aeschylus, Sophocles, Plato, Aristotle, etc. The mathematics tutorial would study Euclid's *Elements*, and the Greek tutorial would emphasize translation from ancient Greek to English. One aim of the Reading and Writing Tutorial, Adler said, "is to teach the student how to read and in so doing to generalize for him the rules of reading in such a way that he learns the basic principles of the liberal arts of grammar, logic and rhetoric. . . ." The student's writing would be "confined, for the most part, to the doing of brief commentaries on very small portions of the text being concurrently read."

A NEW CURRICULUM FOR ST. JOHN'S

In the fall of 1938, Father Virgil began concrete and detailed planning for the new curriculum. On November 16 he wrote a hopeful and confident letter to Adler:

> This is just to let you know that we had our first faculty meeting a few days ago. There were thirty present, which includes some of our clerics about to be ordained, who are greatly interested in the new ideas. As a result, we are going to mimeograph a few pages out of the latest catalogue of St. John's Annapolis, together with the list of books and pass them around with a copy of your nine-page letter of last September. Indications at present are . . . that there is much interest in the program.

Michel recognized that there would be objections to this scheme, but he was optimistic nonetheless. Besides, he told Adler: "There is general agreement that the plan would work best with our ecclesiastical students."

Just a week after writing this letter, Father Virgil became fatally ill. He died on November 26, and his plan for reform of the St. John's curriculum died with him. The plans that he had made had not been adopted by the faculty and without his leadership could not be implemented. What might have occurred in the future at Collegeville can only be surmised from the experience at Annapolis, where St. John's College successfully installed its great-books program and made it permanent.

Soon after Michel's death Mortimer Adler wrote "A Christian Educator," a brilliant tribute to his friend's accomplishments in the field of higher education. Of Michel's ability to fathom the depths of his subject, Adler said:

> Father Virgil Michel was both a teacher and an educator, a teacher who never failed to ask the ultimate questions about the means and ends of his teaching, an educator whose vision of program and policy was always focused by his understanding of the place of learning in human life.[21]

Adler praised Michel's efforts to reform the curriculum at St. John's University; these plans, he wrote, "have momentous significance for the renaissance of Catholic education in this country. . . ."[22]

Despite the efforts of Michel, Adler, and others, great-books programs and similar attempts to return to an authentic liberal education did not sweep the nation. Colleges after Virgil Michel's era by and large continued in the paths that Michel had deplored. Today, fifty years later, the same criticisms are appropriate and the same reforms are needed.

NOTES

1. Virgil Michel, "Utopia Rediviva," in Robert L. Spaeth, ed., *Liberal Education: Essays on the Philosophy of Higher Education* (Collegeville: St. John's University, 1981) 15.

2. Michel, "Utopia Rediviva," *ibid.* 17.

3. Michel, "Utopia Rediviva," *ibid.* 17–18.

4. Michel, "Utopia Rediviva," *ibid.* 24.

5. Michel, "Utopia Rediviva," *ibid.* 19.

6. Michel, "Utopia Rediviva," *ibid.* 20.

7. Michel, "Utopia Rediviva," *ibid.* 21.

8. Michel, "Utopia Rediviva," *ibid.* 21.

9. Michel, "Utopia Rediviva," *ibid.* 22.

10. Michel, "Utopia Rediviva," *ibid.* 23–24.

11. Michel, "Utopia Rediviva," *ibid.* 20–21.

12. Virgil Michel, "Stimulating Intellectual Independence in Senior College Students," in Robert L. Spaeth, ed., *Liberal Education: Essays on the Philosophy of Higher Education* (Collegeville: St. John's University, 1981) 34–35.

13. Michel, "Stimulating Intellectual Independence in Senior College Students," *ibid.* 35.

14. Michel, "Stimulating Intellectual Independence in Senior College Students," *ibid.* 37.

15. Michel, "Stimulating Intellectual Independence in Senior College Students," *ibid.* 39.

16. Michel, "Stimulating Intellectual Independence in Senior College Students," *ibid.* 39–40.

17. Michel, "Utopia Redidiva," *ibid.* 22.

18. Michel, "Utopia Redidiva," *ibid.* 22–23.

19. Michel, "Stimulating Intellectual Independence in Senior College Students," *ibid.* 40.

20. Michel, "Utopia Redidiva," *ibid.* 22; "Stimulating Intellectual Independence in Senior College Students," *ibid.* 40.

21. Mortimer J. Adler, "A Christian Educator," in Robert L. Spaeth, ed., *Liberal Education: Essays on the Philosophy of Higher Education* (Collegeville: St. John's University, 1981) 67.

22. Adler, "A Christian Educator," *ibid.* 68.

9

American Catholic

Since Fr. Virgil Michel's death half a century ago, the United States, the Catholic Church, and the entire world have undergone profound changes. Observed from the 1980s, the era of the 1930s appears to be ancient history. Is it reasonable or even possible to emulate Virgil Michel, who lived in a country, a Church, a world so different from our own? To begin to answer that question requires a comparison of two eras.

Virgil Michel's adult life fell between two world wars, two great watersheds in modern American history. World War I dragged the United States into the maelstrom of international conflict from which it has never emerged. World War II catapulted the United States willy-nilly into the first rank of world powers, and the responsibilities of that position remain with it today.

Between these two wars Americans discovered the excitement as well as the temptations of material prosperity, then suffered the depredations of the Great Depression. The war that President Woodrow Wilson said would "make the world safe for democracy" had given way to a troubled period of peace, a peace that did not last a generation. Even during that war, Soviet communism had seized power in Russia, and in 1933 the menacing Nazi Party led by Adolf Hitler imposed a

Left: Virgil Michel, the fisherman, in 1933.

Right: Virgil Michel before the skeleton of a birch tepee in which he had just celebrated the Eucharist in June 1932.

fascist dictatorship on Germany. Peace as well as war presented grave problems.

When Virgil Michel returned to St. John's from the Red Lake Indian Mission in the fall of 1933, the world he observed must have seemed bleak indeed. At home, the Depression had reached Minnesota in all its force. In the nation as a whole, 15,000,000 people were unemployed. Abroad, Hitler had destroyed democracy in Germany and had begun to create a war machine more threatening than Germany's of the Great War; Josef Stalin had imposed a totalitarianism on the Soviet people cruel enough to compete with Hitler's for the suffering it caused.

The questions such desperate political and economic conditions raised were stark and profound. Was the world destined for more war despite the somber lessons taught by the slaughter of the world war of 1914–1918? Were the freedoms prized so highly in the United States and Europe to be extinguished by the darkness of fascist and communist totalitarianism? Was the West's economic system, once promising to alleviate centuries-old poverty, capable only of instability and the imposing of material hardship? And if material prosperity could be brought back, were people capable any longer of resisting the allure of a materialist life that could destroy spiritual values?

A NATION IN CRISIS

Taken together, the grim facts of national and international life constituted a major crisis for the people of the United States in the 1930s. The international crisis struck Europe first but the United States could only support and finally join the Allied forces fighting the Axis powers of Germany, Italy and finally Japan. As the war clouds gathered, economic depression at home continued to threaten and damage lives and communities.

President Franklin D. Roosevelt, in his inaugural address of March 4, 1933, described the United States as "a stricken Nation in the midst of a stricken world." The new president named the fearsome conditions prevailing in the country:

> Values have shrunk to fantastic levels; taxes have risen; our ability to pay has fallen; government of all kinds is faced by serious curtailment of income; the means of exchange are frozen in the currents of trade; the withered leaves of industrial enterprise lie on every side; farmers find no markets for their produce; the savings of many years in thousands of families are gone. . . . More important, a host of unemployed citizens face the grim problem of existence, and an equally great number toil with little return.[1]

Roosevelt was nonetheless determined to attack the nation's plight with confidence in its economic and political system. "Our Constitution is so simple and practical," he said, "that it is possible always to meet extraordinary needs by changes in emphasis and arrangement without loss of essential form."[2]

In Minnesota the following year Governor Floyd B. Olson looked forward to more radical changes. Speaking to the delegates of the 1934 convention of his party, Governor Olson said:

> The ultimate goal of the Farmer-Labor Party is a cooperative commonwealth wherein government will stifle as much as possible the greed and avarice of the private profit system and will bring about a more equitable distribution of the wealth produced by the hands and minds of the people.[3]

Evidence at home and abroad accumulated in those early years of the 1930s that radical changes might be imminent in politics and economics. This was the world Virgil Michel lived in for the last five years of his life, which turned out to be his most productive years.

A CHURCH OF TRADITION

If *crisis* is the word best describing the condition for the secular world in Virgil Michel's time, the single word fitting the condition of the Catholic Church might be *tradition*. Catholics the world over, American Catholics included, adhered to traditions of worship and belief that were centuries old. Latin was the language of the liturgy. The sixteenth-century Council of Trent determined the formulation of Catholic principles of faith and morals. The nineteenth-century Vatican Council I had solidified the authority of bishops and pope and declared the pope infallible when speaking *ex cathedra* on matters of faith and morals.

American Catholics in the 1930s were emerging from their condition as immigrants and becoming fully Americanized. Perhaps more than other national groups of Catholics, they rarely departed from the beliefs and practices that time and authority had honored. Their religious life tended to be separate from their secular life, and although Catholics suffered as much as any Americans from the secular crisis of the times, their religion was rarely injected into secular problems. Historians have called this "the era of devotional Catholicism." Although the reform movements organized in response to the Depression included some Catholic leaders, it was also true, as historian Jay P. Dolan has written, "of the more than thirty-three thousand priests in the United States at that time, the vast majority were more interested in novenas than labor unions."[4]

SECULAR AND RELIGIOUS LIFE TODAY

Half a century after Virgil Michel, both secular society and the Catholic Church appear to have been greatly transformed. In the 1980s the United States has enjoyed unprecedented prosperity, and with it suffers from the accompanying materialism that eats away at spiritual life. Moreover, the post-World War II age has been characterized by a lowering of traditional moral standards. Disintegrating family life is measured by divorce statistics; lax sexual mores are demonstrated by the numbers of teen-age pregnancies; social injustice is visible in the growing numbers of homeless people; moral decline in politics and business is revealed by recurrent scandals.

World War II left the international world divided into two hostile camps—American and Soviet. The tensions of these camps have been accompanied by the acquisition on both sides of vast systems of nuclear weapons. Whenever wars or conflicts have occurred—such as in Vietnam or the Middle East—the awful possibilities of a nuclear war have terrified the world. And although the United Nations has tried for over four decades to induce sovereign nations to adjust their differences through negotiation rather than violence, the world remains a tinder box of conflict.

Although the facts are quite different from those of the 1930s, the most accurate name for the secular world's condition in the 1980s remains "crisis." For the United States and other industrialized nations, the crisis is more political than economic; for the developing nations, poverty is the true crisis.

In the Catholic Church the stable system of traditional devotional beliefs and practices was radically changed by Vatican Council II. Although the bishops of the Council aimed to update certain aspects of the Church—such as introducing vernacular languages into the liturgy—the results went far deeper. Instability struck the Catholic Church for the first time in centuries, and the shock waves hit American Catholics hard. Priests and sisters by the thousand left their vocation; Catholic school enrollment plummeted; the authority of pope and bishop was repeatedly challenged; dissent from received teaching became commonplace. The catchword for Catholics was no longer "tradition" but "change."

It is conventional wisdom today that there can be no return to a world without nuclear weapons and no return for Catholics to the conditions of life before Vatican II. If the Catholic faith is to have any salutary effect on people today, it must admit that the Church is a new Church, and it must cope with conditions hitherto unknown in the world. What place, then, can Virgil Michel—an American Catholic of the pre-war era—have in the 1980s?

VIRGIL MICHEL'S EXAMPLE

Virgil Michel, as this book has shown, believed that the faith of a Catholic, understood well and practiced diligently, provides a basis for reform of the conditions of crisis in the secular world. His work can be described as an effort to make the Catholic tradition alive in the modern world and to spread Christian life into a world whose crisis was as much spiritual as material.

No arena of human activity escaped Father Virgil's interest and attention. Today a scanning of his surviving correspondence shows he paid heed to The Single Tax League of Texas, The Catholic Conference on Industrial Problems, The Cooperative League, the National Catholic Welfare Conference, the National Catholic Rural Life Conference, The Friends of Brownson, The Catholic Worker, The Catholic Dramatic Movement, etc.

To the extent that Virgil Michel let no human concern escape his discerning eye, his example can apply to any era. But can one go further and imagine Virgil Michel's response, in particular, to our world, the world of the 1980s?

How would Virgil Michel understand the crisis in modern secular society—rampant materialism, the gap between rich and poor, decaying morality, the threat of nuclear war? Judging from his response to conditions in the 1930s, he might well look for an underlying cause, and once again he might say it is the loss of spiritual guidance in people's lives. Michel's habit of digging beneath a problem would be especially useful today, when so many analyses of modern life, often superficial, often inconsistent with one another, are offered from all sides.

The problems characteristic of our era cry out for a spiritual analysis, for material prosperity has been the source of deep problems as well as a solution to others. Why do wealth and leisure not bring happiness? Why do moral virtues fall apart among people whose lives viewed materially seem so desirable? How can there be homeless people in a society so wealthy? Surely, Virgil Michel would say, the life of the soul in modern people must lack something essential to a decent life. And it would be likely that he would turn again to the Christian liturgy for a source of spiritual energy and to the worshiping community as a model of community life.

If Virgil Michel were here today to observe the massive confrontation of the American and Soviet systems, the competition for the mind of humankind between capitalism and communism, he might well once again call for a middle way. Near the end of his life Michel wrote an article with the subtitle "Between Communism and Fascism Lies the Christian Plan for Social Reconstruction."[5] Between communism and capitalism Michel also found Christianity to be a desirable middle way. As the capitalism-communism competition today is a more deadly version of that already begun before World War II, Michel might offer the same solution today with even more conviction.

How would Virgil Michel cope with the post-Vatican II Church? Since the Council adopted many of Michel's ideas about liturgical reform, he would no doubt find the Catholic liturgy more prepared than in his own time to do its work in the wider community. Yet there is scant evidence that the liturgy is effective today in the ways Michel called for. Although many parishes today operate programs of community service, particularly anti-poverty programs, the translation of community worship into community action remains an elusive ideal in the American Catholic Church. Michel's gifts for proposing practical remedies for visible problems could once again be used in liturgical studies.

What resistance prevents the liturgy from transforming the members of a parish into the socially-minded community so badly needed? Michel saw in his day that better understanding of the liturgy as well as its reform were needed. These changes have in large part been one of the celebrated accomplishments of Vatican II. Yet something is still missing.

What Michel wanted the liturgical spirit to overcome in his time was a corrosive individualism. It could be plausibly argued today that individualism has become more widespread and more damaging to community values in the intervening years than half a century ago. Thus Virgil Michel might criticize the liturgy less and recognize its adversary as more formidable today. The American bishops in 1986 noted that the United States "prides itself on both its competitive sense of initiative and its spirit of teamwork," but they added:

> Today a greater spirit of partnership and teamwork is needed; competition alone will not do the job. It has too many negative consequences for family life, the economically vulnerable, and the environment. Only a renewed commitment by all to

the common good can deal creatively with the realities of international interdependence and economic dislocations in the domestic economy.[6]

SOCIAL ENCYCLICALS

For guidance in his thinking about the problems of human communities, Michel often turned to the social encyclicals. In his lifetime, two such papal letters stood out, *Rerum novarum* by Pope Leo XIII and *Quadragesimo anno* by Pope Pius XI. These encyclicals, one might say, provided the basic analysis of the societies on which the liturgy needed to work.

The tradition of social encyclicals has expanded since Virgil Michel, particularly during the papacies of John XXIII and Paul VI. Both *Mater et magistra* and *Pacem in terris* of Pope John, but particularly the former, continue the kind of social analysis that Michel favored. A similar statement might be made about Pope Paul's letter *Populorum progressio* and Pope John Paul II's encyclical *Sollicitudo rei socialis.*

In the United States in the 1980s, the National Conference of Catholic Bishops began to issue carefully considered pastoral letters on social issues. *The Challenge of Peace* on the moral problems associated with nuclear weaponry, and *Economic Justice for All* applying Catholic social teaching to the contemporary American economy, attempt what Michel constantly tried, to get to the bottom of social problems and to offer solutions to them inspired by Catholic tradition. It is very probable that Virgil Michel today might applaud these efforts, though it is difficult to say whether he could agree with all their details.

But papal encyclicals and episcopal letters speak to a Church far more diverse than the American Catholic Church of the 1930s. Although Michel would no doubt have welcomed the expanded role for the laity that Vatican II encouraged—and the popular metaphor for the universal Church, "the people of God" that replaced "the Mystical Body of Christ"—the laity in America grew less and less unified in the years after Vatican II. Some of the pluralism of opinion was political, but as the American bishops entered the policy debate on nuclear arms and the economy, the various views of Catholics on public policy seemed also to be varying views on the social teaching of the Church. But pluralism also emerged on teachings closer to the heart of Catholicism, moral teachings in particular. National polls regularly revealed that large percentages of American Catholics disagreed with the teachings of their Church in both theory and practice on issues such as birth control and divorce.

Virgil Michel in the 1980s would probably not wish to be associated with any faction in the Catholic Church. In his own time he did not identify himself as liberal or conservative, but it is difficult for Catholic thinkers today to escape such labeling. Perhaps Michel today would seek to be guided once again by the social encyclicals and from this platform speak to Catholics of all factions that have emerged since the Council. The American bishops seem to have attempted this in their pastoral letters of the 1980s, but they nonetheless found themselves criticized for joining one or another of the existing American Catholic factions. Possibly Virgil Michel's special genius for clear communication would provide a missing element in today's Catholic leadership.

FATHER VIRGIL IN OUR TIME

How can Virgil Michel's thoughts, as we find them in his writings and other accomplishments, be brought to bear on the issues of our time? It would be a mistake to try to guess at what his opinions would be today concerning this or that modern problem. What would Virgil Michel think about nuclear disarmament? about liberation theology? about the preferential option for the poor? These are unanswerable questions and in any case not the right questions to ask about the potential influence of Virgil Michel today.

Rather than creating a myth about Virgil Michel in the 1980s, we should attempt to recover the spirit of Virgil Michel's approach to the world and infuse it into our own thinking. But can the spirit of Virgil Michel be defined without reference to his age? Was he a "product of his time" or was he "a man for all seasons"? Such a question always arises in the study of important people of the past and is especially important when the historical person is someone as admirable as Father Virgil.

This book has emphasized Virgil Michel's warnings about the dangers of individualism and his conviction of the benefits of community life, both for the Church and the secular world. Long before Virgil Michel, individualism had been understood to be a pervasive American tendency. Alexis de Tocqueville, an acute observer who visited the United States in the 1830s, defined it as follows:

> Individualism is a calm and considered feeling which disposes each citizen to isolate himself from the mass of his fellows and withdraw into the circle of family and friends; with this little society formed to his taste, he gladly leaves the greater society to look after itself.[7]

Michel understood individualism in the same way Tocqueville did—and he quoted the same passage from *Democracy in America* to introduce his 1936 essay "Modern Individualism and Its Social Effects." In much of his writing and teaching, this dangerous kind of individualism stood at the center of Michel's concerns about life in the United States.

The individual will always stand in some problematic relationship to communities of persons. The welfare of one person is not always served by the same actions as the welfare of a parish or city or nation. And within each person is the desire to serve oneself, probably a stronger will than the desire to be of service to others. Individualism as a tendency to help oneself can of course be salutary, but individualism as understood by Tocqueville and Virgil Michel needs to be fought against because it tends to serve the individual at the expense of the group.

Individualism cannot destroy community life, but at the least it sets up a tension, between a life devoted to oneself and a life devoted to one's society, local or national. This tension is as old as history itself. It appears in various forms in economic life, politics, the parish, and schools. When individualism is recognized as a danger, sometimes extreme solutions, such as collectivism, are proposed that are worse than the problem itself. Every age must recognize for itself where the central problem lies, and where on the spectrum of dispositions between extreme individualism and extreme collectivism are found contemporary people and their problems. Virgil Michel of course would also have us ask, what does our Christian faith say about the current situation?

Individualism has remained a powerful American trait to our own time. Some would say it has been strengthened. Today it is necessary once again to remind ourselves that the only values to be set against the dangerous force of individualism are the values of community. The central value of any community, religious or secular, is the common good. Much of Virgil Michel's work was a search for the meaning of the common good in theory and practice, in communities of all sorts. Since that meaning continues to elude us today, it is safe to conclude that were Virgil Michel alive today, his search for the common good would continue unabated. To emulate his example, we can do no less.

NOTES

1. *The Year of Crisis: The Public Papers and Addresses of Franklin D. Roosevelt,* II (New York: Random House, 1938) 15, 11.

2. *The Year of Crisis, ibid.* 14–15.

3. John S. McGrath and James J. Delmont, *Floyd Björnsterne Olson: Minnesota's Greatest Liberal Governor* (St. Paul, Minnesota, 1937) 246.

4. Jay P. Dolan, *The American Catholic Experience: A History from Colonial Times to the Present* (Garden City, N.Y.: Doubleday and Co., 1985) 406.

5. Virgil Michel, "Social Reconstruction: Between Communism and Fascism Lies the Christian Plan for Social Reconstruction," *Michaelman* 4 (1939) 2.

6. National Conference of Catholic Bishops, *Economic Justice for All: Pastoral Letter on Catholic Social Teaching and the U. S. Economy* (Washington: United States Catholic Conference, 1986) para. 296.

7. Alexis de Tocqueville, *Democracy in America* (Garden City, N.Y.: Doubleday and Co., 1969) 506.

Bibliographical Essay

A great deal of value is still contained in Virgil Michel's own words which speak with great clarity across the years. He was a man who did not hide his ideas under a bushel but wrote voluminously; books, essays, pamphlets, brochures, reviews, and articles poured from his pen. Yet virtually all of these writings have become unavailable. How can contemporary readers gain access to the thought of Virgil Michel and pursue further details of the life presented in these pages?

The Office of Academic Affairs of St. John's University has made seventeen major essays on education and social justice available in two collections edited by Robert L. Spaeth:

Liberal Education: Essays on the Philosophy of Higher Education by Fr. Virgil Michel, O.S.B. (Collegeville: St. John's University, 1981) contains "A Religious Need of the Day" (1925), "Utopia Rediviva" (1926), "Are We Educating Moral Parasites?" (1927), "Stimulating Intellectual Independence in Senior College Students" (1927), "The Basic Need of Christian Education Today" (1929), "The Need Today of College Courses in Political Science" (1935), and "Let's Examine Ourselves" (1938). The volume concludes with Mortimer J. Adler's essay on Virgil Michel, "A Christian Educator" (1939).

The Social Question: Essays on Capitalism and Christianity by Fr. Virgil Michel, O.S.B. (Collegeville: St. John's University, 1987) includes "The Liturgy the Basis of Social Regeneration" (1935), "Individualism and Its Social Effects" (1936), "The Nature of Capitalism" (1936), "The Common Good" (1937), "Critique of Capitalism" (1937), "Government Regulation of Business" (1937), "The Mystical Body and Economic Justice" (1938), "Agriculture and Reconstruction" (1939),

"Christian Culture" (1939), and "The Bourgeois Spirit and the Christian Renewal" (1940).

In addition, "The Liturgy the Basis of Social Regeneration" is reprinted with an introduction and bibliography in Patrick W. Carey, ed., *American Catholic Religious Thought* (New York: Paulist Press, 1987) 273–83. "The Scope of the Liturgical Movement" (1936) is reprinted in Paul Marx, *Virgil Michel and the Liturgical Movement* (Collegeville: The Liturgical Press, 1957) 439–43.

No parallel collection on liturgy or the laity exists; these writings must be gathered from scattered sources. For Virgil Michel on the liturgy, see *Why the Mass?* (Collegeville: The Liturgical Press, 1928), *The Liturgical Movement* (Collegeville: The Liturgical Press, 1930), "The Scope of the Liturgical Movement," *Orate Fratres* X (1936) 485–90, *The Liturgy of the Church* (New York: Macmillan, 1937), and "The Social Nature of the Offertory and the Social Nature of Communion," *The Mystical Body and Social Justice* (Collegeville: St. John's Abbey, 1938) 5–16. On the laity: "Layman in the Church," *Commonweal* XII (1930) 123–25, "Baptismal Consciousness," *Orate Fratres* I (1927) 309–13, "Catholic Leadership and the College," *Orate Fratres* X (1935) 22–27, "A Layman's Lament," *Orate Fratres* XII (1937) 80–84, "Will Anti-Clericalism Increase in the United States?" *Ecclesiastical Review* XCVI (1937) 284–90, "Christian Woman," *Orate Fratres* XIII (1939) 248–56.

Readers interested in the issues surrounding Christian social reconstruction will want to find Virgil Michel's book *Christian Social Reconstruction* (Milwaukee: Bruce, 1937) and the following lengthy pamphlets all published in 1936 by the Wanderer Printing Company of St. Paul: *Human Rights, Ideals of Reconstruction, Labor and Industry, Money and the Common Good, The Nature of Capitalism, Ownership, Reconstruction Schemes, St. Thomas and Today,* and *The Theory of State.*

The archives of St. John's Abbey contain unpublished manuscripts of Virgil Michel which will be of interest to some. Among those can be found: "Christian Education for Rural

Living," "Liturgical Movement and Catholic Women," "Liturgy and Catholic Life," "Liturgy and Labor," and "The Philosophical and Theological Bases of the Liturgical Movement."

Any further study of Virgil Michel's life must begin with Jeremy Hall, *The Full Stature of Christ: The Ecclesiology of Virgil Michel, O.S.B.* (Collegeville: The Liturgical Press, 1976) and Paul Marx, *Virgil Michel and the Liturgical Movement* (Collegeville: The Liturgical Press, 1957). Both Hall and Marx include complete bibliographies of works by and about Virgil Michel.

A notable earlier collection of essays on Virgil Michel appeared in the January 1939 issue of *Orate Fratres* with articles by William Busch on liturgy, Sr. Jane Marie Murray on education, Theodore C. Vermilye on ecumenism, Gerald B. Phelan on philosophy, Mortimer Adler on education, Aloisius Muench on rural issues, Alphonse J. Matt on social issues, and Dorothy Day on social action.

The following are worthwhile articles or pamphlets on specific and significant aspects of Virgil Michel's life and work: Leo R. Ward and Emerson Hynes, "Virgil Michel," *Commonweal* 29 (1938) 237-38, Emerson Hynes, "Social Thought of Virgil Michel," *American Catholic Sociological Review* I (1940) 172-80, Jeremy Hall, "The American Liturgical Movement: The Early Years," *Worship* L (1976) 472-89, Paul R. Messgarger, "Midwestern Catholicism: Two Portraits," *Listening* XI (1976) 22-32, "Come, Let Us Reminisce . . . ," *Popular Liturgical Library: Golden Anniversary Catalog* (Collegeville: The Liturgical Press, 1976) 2-6, Catherine de Hueck Doherty, "Dom Virgil Michel," *Not Without Parables* (Notre Dame, Ind: Ave Maria Press, 1977) 104-107, John J. Egan, *Liturgy and Justice: An Unfinished Agenda* (Collegeville: The Liturgical Press, 1983), Mathew A. Ahmann, "Views of a Social Activist," *U.S. Catholic Historian* 2 (1986) 225-27, M. Francis Mannion, "Liturgy and the Present Crisis of Culture," *Worship* LXII (1988) 98-122, and Aidan Kavanagh, "Spirituality in the American Church: An Evaluative Essay," *Contemporary*

Catholicism in the United States, ed. Philip Gleason (Notre Dame, Ind.: Notre Dame University Press, 1969) 197–214.

Two M.A. theses on Michel have been completed in the last decade: Doug Mullin, "Virgil Michel and the Liturgical Revival: Implications for Religious Education" (St. John's University, 1981) and David M. Beaudoin, "Virgil Michel's Application of the Philosophy of Personalism to his Theory of Religious Education" (Marquette University, 1987).

The entire issue of *Worship* for May 1988 is devoted to Virgil Michel and contains these articles: R. W. Franklin, "Virgil Michel: An Introduction," 194–201, Kenneth R. Hines, "Eucharist and Justice: Assessing the Legacy of Virgil Michel," 201–24, Joseph P. Chinnici, "Virgil Michel and the Tradition of Affective Prayer," 225–36, and David M. Beaudoin, "A Personalist Approach to Catechetics," 237–49.

For the American Liturgical Movement after Virgil Michel, see as an introduction H. A. Reinhold, "The Liturgical Movement To Date," *Christ's Sacrifice and Ours* (Boston: Liturgical Conference, 1948), William Busch, "Past, Present and Future," *Orate Fratres* XXV (October–November, 1951), William J. Leonard, ed., *Liturgy for the People: Essays in Honor of Gerald Ellard, S. J.* (Milwaukee: Bruce, 1963), Frederick A. McManus, ed., *The Revival of the Liturgy* (New York: Herder and Herder, 1963), Godfrey Diekmann, "Is There a Distinct American Contribution to the Liturgical Renewal?," *Worship* XLV (1971) 578–87, Aelred Tegels, "Fifty Years of *Worship,*" *Worship* L (1976) 466–71, Colman J. Barry, *Worship and Work: St. John's Abbey and University 1856–1980* (Collegeville: St. John's Abbey, 1980), Aidan Kavanagh, "Liturgical and Credal Studies," *A Century of Church History,* ed. Henry Bowden, (Carbondale, Ill.: Southern Illinois University Press, 1988) 216–44, and essays by John Tracy Ellis, Andrew M. Greeley, Robert W. Hovda, Eugene J. McCarthy, James O'Gara, Albert C. Outler, and Jaroslav Pelikan in Colman J. Barry and Robert L. Spaeth, eds, *A Sense of Place: Saint John's of Collegeville* (Collegeville: St. John's University, 1987).

R. W. FRANKLIN is associate professor of history and director of the Christian Humanism Project at St. John's University, Collegeville, Minnesota. He has written *Nineteenth Century Churches: The History of a New Catholicism in Württemberg, England, and France* (Garland, 1987), *Readings in Christian Humanism* (Augsburg, 1982), *New Essays in Christian Humanism* (St. John's University, 1984), and a series of articles on the nineteenth-century liturgical movement in *Worship* from 1975 to 1985.

ROBERT L. SPAETH has been dean of the College of Arts and Sciences at St. John's University, Collegeville, Minnesota, since 1979. He is the author of *No Easy Answers: Christians Debate Nuclear Arms* (Harper & Row/Winston, 1983), *The Church and a Catholic's Conscience* (Harper & Row/Winston, 1985), and *Exhortations on Liberal Education: A Dean Speaks His Mind* (St. John's University, 1988).